Spreadsheet Safe™

Training Manual

Syllabus Version 1.0

First edition May 2008

ISBN 9780 7517 5343 1

British Library Cataloguing-in-Publication Data
A catalogue record for this book
is available from the British Library

Published by

BPP Learning Media Ltd
BPP House, Aldine Place
London W12 8AA

www.bpp.com/learningmedia

CONTENTS

What is Spreadsheet Safe™?

Spreadsheet Safe™ is an innovative training and certification programme designed to help organisations and spreadsheet end-users assure and maintain the highest standards in spreadsheet design, usage and control.

The programme was developed by Q-Validus, an international certification solutions provider, in conjunction with its training and testing partners, BPP Learning Media and BTL Learning & Assessment.

Spreadsheet Safe is a total solution providing training materials, testing and certification.

Visit www.spreadsheetsafe.com for further details.

Scottish Qualifications Authority (SQA) endorsement

The Spreadsheet Safe™ qualification is currently in the final stages of Scottish Qualifications Authority (SQA) endorsement.

Which version of Microsoft Excel?

The material in this book is based on Microsoft Excel 2003. At the time of publication, this was still the most widely used spreadsheet package.

A version of the Spreadsheet Safe™ programme covering Microsoft Excel 2007 is planned for release towards the end of 2008.

Spreadsheet Safe™ e-learning material

The Spreadsheet Safe™ programme includes e-learning material that provides on-screen delivery of the main points from each of the five chapters in the Spreadsheet Safe™ book.

Visit www.spreadsheetsafe.com to access the e-learning content.

Programme goals

Spreadsheet Safe™ is a certificate programme to help spreadsheet end-users and organisations manage and maintain safe spreadsheets.

Candidates shall be able to setup, arrange and present their spreadsheets based on standard best practices in spreadsheet design, end-use and control.

Spreadsheet Safe™ candidates shall achieve well set out, error-free spreadsheets, which show a clear history and ownership path.

Candidates shall also be able check their work for input accuracy, breaking down formulas into smaller more auditable parts, as well as making units of measure explicit for ease of update.

Spreadsheet Safe™ candidates shall routinely check their work for calculation and output accuracy, as well creating and validating formulas.

Candidates shall also recognise common spreadsheet errors.

Spreadsheet Safe™ candidates shall be able to create charts, and choose the most suitable chart types in order to illustrate data accurately and to enhance meaning.

Candidates are required to work in an informed and responsible way, and to appreciate the importance of spreadsheet review, audit and validation.

Spreadsheet Safe™ candidates shall also be aware that spreadsheets may be auditable as part of regulatory requirements.

Candidates shall also have due regard to pertinent Health and Safety issues with regard to using computers.

Spreadsheet Safe™ helps candidates demonstrate their skill and awareness in working carefully and productively with spreadsheets.

The full syllabus is shown on the following pages.

Spreadsheet Safe™ Syllabus (Version 1.0) Copyright © Q-Validus 2008

Category	Skill area	Ref.	Measuring point
1.1 SETUP	*1.1.1 Prepare*	1.1.1.1	Determine that a spreadsheet application is fit for the proposed purpose.
		1.1.1.2	State spreadsheet purpose clearly, and indicate any assumptions.
		1.1.1.3	List the requirements. Give the author name, change history, version number.
		1.1.1.4	Set, examine spreadsheet file properties.
		1.1.1.5	Set out any conventions used, such as calculation methods or functions, the meaning of formatting and styles.
		1.1.1.6	Recognise that spreadsheet data formats such as formats for dates, numbers and codes should be explicit, appropriate and applied consistently.
	1.1.2 Organise	1.1.2.1	Lay out spreadsheet content logically and coherently over a clearly organised worksheet scheme.
		1.1.2.2	Recognise the value of using a summary or index worksheet to help users navigate and understand the organisation of the spreadsheet.
		1.1.2.3	Save, backup and verify distinct spreadsheet versions.
		1.1.2.4	Apply strong password protection, using mixed case, and non-alphanumeric characters (at least 8) to protect against unauthorised access.
		1.1.2.5	Recognise different macro security levels in spreadsheets and apply appropriately.
1.2 INPUTS	*1.2.1 Controls*	1.2.1.1	Place a single instance of a given constant (eg conversion or tax rates) in separate cells.
		1.2.1.2	Break down more complex formulas into smaller component parts to help with readability, comprehension, and for ease of update.
		1.2.1.3	Apply named ranges to make formulas more manageable.
		1.2.1.4	Use manual and automatic calculation modes.
	1.2.2 Integrity	1.2.2.1	Make units of measure explicit.
		1.2.2.2	Apply the precision as displayed setting.
		1.2.2.3	Import fixed length or delimited text file (eg CSV) into a spreadsheet and validate that the data types are correct.
		1.2.2.4	Reconcile the integrity of data from external sources as complete, consistent and correct.

Category	Skill area	Ref.	Measuring point
1.3 CALCULATE	*1.3.1 Formulas*	1.3.1.1	Use mathematical and logical formulas and functions in a spreadsheet.
		1.3.1.2	Correct the order of precedence in mathematical operators.
		1.3.1.3	Understand the concept of circular references in a spreadsheet. Recognise and remove circular references.
		1.3.1.4	Recognise array (matrix) formulas in spreadsheets.
		1.3.1.5	Check number and type of function arguments (Lookup function).
		1.3.1.6	Check for and correct relative, absolute and mixed cell references.
		1.3.1.7	Create worksheet, spreadsheet links, and validate that they summarise, update correctly, and are complete.
	1.3.2 Errors	1.3.2.1	Check for missing input values.
		1.3.2.2	Check for and correct missing precedent cells.
		1.3.2.3	Apply ISERROR, ISNA functions.
		1.3.2.4	Correct #DIV/0! occurrences where appropriate.
		1.3.2.5	Check for and correct ####, #VALUE!, #NAME, #REF!, #NUM!, error values.
	1.3.3 Totals	1.3.3.1	Create cross-totals as a way to validate totalling.
		1.3.3.2	Check for and correct errors in totalling caused by row, column insertion or deletion.
		1.3.3.3	Check for and correct double counted sub-total errors.
		1.3.3.4	Check for and correct mismatched cross-totals.
		1.3.3.5	Check for and correct automatic sum total errors.
1.4 OUTPUT	*1.4.1 Data*	1.4.1.1	Show hidden data by changing custom formats (font or background colour), hidden zero values.
		1.4.1.2	Distinguish format decimal commands and round functions.
		1.4.1.3	Apply format decimal commands, round functions.
		1.4.1.4	Export data as CSV, tab or other file format, and validate as correct.
		1.4.1.5	Print and proof spreadsheet outputs.
	1.4.2 Charts	1.4.2.1	Create a chart based on source data.
		1.4.2.2	Switch between different chart types.
		1.4.2.3	Check the orientation of a chart so that all data series are visible.
		1.4.2.4	Apply appropriate chart axes, orientation, scales, titles and annotation to enhance chart meaning.
		1.4.2.5	Express data in a chart meaningfully by choosing an appropriate chart type.

Category	Skill area	Ref.	Measuring point
1.5 AUDIT	*1.5.1 Review*	1.5.1.1	Understand how spreadsheet criticality, risk and potential business impact determine the extent of review and control requirements.
		1.5.1.2	Submit the spreadsheet for independent review, approval before circulation.
		1.5.1.3	Recognise the need for periodic re-review.
		1.5.1.4	Run and validate test cases, with typical and extreme values, for all calculations.
		1.5.1.5	Check outputs using alternate calculation methods.
		1.5.1.6	Un-hide rows, columns, worksheets.
		1.5.1.7	Un-hide formulas.
		1.5.1.8	Inspect formulas for logic and output accuracy.
		1.5.1.9	Recognise the presence of advanced features in a spreadsheet such as macros and pivot tables.
	1.5.2 Validation	1.5.2.1	Use IF function to test for call values being within expected ranges.
		1.5.2.2	Review for data type mis-entry (eg text entry for numeric characters.).
		1.5.2.3	Apply conditional formatting to highlight errors.
		1.5.2.4	Apply validation criteria: values, whole numbers, and decimals.
		1.5.2.5	Apply validation criteria: date, time, character lengths.
		1.5.2.6	Apply custom validation criteria.
	1.5.3 Laws & Guidelines	1.5.3.1	Be aware of data protection legislation or conventions in your country.
		1.5.3.2	Be aware that spreadsheets may need to be controlled as part of regulatory requirements.
		1.5.3.3	Recognise that spreadsheets may be controlled records and subject to archive requirements in legislation.
		1.5.3.4	Recognise the significance of disability / equality legislation in helping to provide all users with access to information.

1 SETUP

Measuring points

▸ Determine that a spreadsheet application is fit for the proposed purpose.
▸ State the spreadsheet purpose clearly and indicate any assumptions.
▸ List the spreadsheet requirements. Give the author name, change history and version number.
▸ Set and examine spreadsheet file properties.
▸ Set out any conventions used, such as calculation methods or functions, the meaning of formatting and styles.
▸ Recognise that spreadsheet data formats such as formats for dates, numbers and codes should be explicit, appropriate and applied consistently.
▸ Lay out spreadsheet content logically and coherently over a clearly organised worksheet scheme.
▸ Recognise the value of using a summary or index worksheet to help users navigate and understand the organisation of the spreadsheet.
▸ Save, backup and verify distinct spreadsheet versions.
▸ Apply strong password protection to spreadsheets, using mixed case and non-alphanumeric characters (at least 8) to protect against unauthorised access.
▸ Recognise different macro security levels in spreadsheets and apply appropriately.

SPREADSHEET SAFE™

| **Setup** | Input controls | Calculate | Output | Audit |

The right tool?

Spreadsheet software is extremely flexible. This is an advantage in that it allows spreadsheets to be developed to meet a wide range of different needs. It can also be a disadvantage, as it may encourage the development of a spreadsheet to meet a need that would be better met by a different application.

Because spreadsheet software is so flexible it is very difficult to identify a single set of circumstances that encompass all situations suited to spreadsheet use. It's slightly easier to identify situations not suited to a spreadsheet application.

Before development starts, ask yourself whether a (cost-effective) specific software application exists that would be better suited to the task. During the spreadsheet development process, if you find the spreadsheet is becoming cumbersome, or requires excessive development, it's likely a more appropriate tool exists.

Examples of specific applications that may be more suited to tasks sometimes tackled by spreadsheets include:

- A database
- Accounting system report writing module
- A production system (including timesheets, inventory management etc.)
- Project management application
- A forecasting/budgeting system

Documentation

What information should be recorded?

Information relating to the purpose, use and content of a spreadsheet should be recorded (documented). This information should include:

- Spreadsheet purpose
- User requirements
- Author
- Version and release history
- Assumptions and conventions used

The level of detail required will vary. A relatively simple spreadsheet will require less detailed documentation than a complex spreadsheet model.

Spreadsheet purpose

The purpose of a spreadsheet should be stated in a clear, concise statement.

The statement should explain what the spreadsheet does and the part it plays in the organisation. It provides a useful starting point for anyone trying to understand what the spreadsheet 'is for' (perhaps someone looking at the file for the first time).

Comments:	Purpose - To show first half yearly sales by magazine and region

Here's an example statement of purpose held in the spreadsheet file properties (covered later in this chapter).

User requirements

User requirements should be established, clarified and documented at an early stage of the spreadsheet design process.

Every spreadsheet is created to meet the needs of a user or a group of users. To ensure the spreadsheet does this successfully, these needs must be documented and understood. The documented user requirements should clearly define what the user requires the spreadsheet to do.

The requirements provide a checklist for the testing process, and ultimately for user acceptance of the completed spreadsheet project. Larger, more complex projects are likely to have more complex user requirements – which will require more detailed documentation held in separate document files.

Author

The author is the person responsible for maintaining the spreadsheet design or structure.

The author maintains the spreadsheet, ensuring it continues to operate as intended. The current author may or may not be the person who originally set up the spreadsheet. Likewise, the author may or may not be a user of the spreadsheet, so may or may not be responsible for updating data held in the file.

Version and release history

'Version' refers to a particular state or stage of design in the development of a spreadsheet. A 'release' is a version that has been issued (released) for use.

If changes are made to formulas or to the structure of the spreadsheet, a new version should be created – so the file should be saved using a name that incorporates a separate version reference. Some versions may be saved to provide a development history, even though they are never released to users.

Version history data should be recorded in a separate worksheet or document. The data held should include the version number, the file name, author, the release date (if released) and a brief comment summarising any changes made.

Microsoft Excel - Fcast2008_VerHistory.xls

File   Edit   View   Insert   Format   Tools   Data   Window   Help   Adobe PDF

	A	B	C	D	E	F
1	Version history					
2						
3	Version	File name	Author	Released?	Release date	Description
4	0.1	Fcast2008_ver01.xls	John Rush	No	10-May-07	Initial design circulated to key finance staff for views
5	0.5	Fcast2008_ver02.xls	John Rush	No	30-May-07	Revised version used for testing
6	1.0	Fcast2008_rel1.0.xls	John Rush	Yes	02-Jun-07	Corrected, tested version issued to department heads
7	1.1	Fcast2008_rel1.1.xls	Ian Barnes	Yes	05-Jul-07	Changed sales classifications per sales director
8	1.2	Fcast2008_rel1.2.xls	Ian Barnes	Yes	01-Sep-07	Figures amended per financal controller
9	2.0	Fcast2008_rel2.0.xls	Ian Barnes	Yes	15-Dec-07	All figures received and agreed; forecast finalised

Release details should be included in the spreadsheet header or footer. This enables users reading a hard-copy to easily identify the release used to create the information they are viewing.

Assumptions and conventions

Assumptions

All assumptions that data within a spreadsheet are based upon should be stated clearly.

Assumptions should be recorded together, in the same area of the spreadsheet. This facilitates quick and easy review, and reduces the risk of an outdated or incorrect assumption being overlooked. The source(s) of data, and factors that would cause the assumptions to change should also be recorded.

A simple example of stating an assumption would be detailing current commission bands and rates in a spreadsheet designed to calculate commission payable to salespeople.

	A	B	C	D
1	**Assumptions**	**Band (£)**	**Rate**	
2	Commission band 1	0 - 5,000	10.0%	
3	Commission band 2	5001 - 10,000	12.5%	
4	Commission band 3	10,001 - 20,000	15.0%	
5	Commission band 4	Over 20,000	20.0%	
6				
7	No upper limit applies - confirmed with Dave Watson September 23 2007			
8	Next review of bands/rates expected January 2008			

Data sources

Data sources should be noted to enable figures to be verified.

Data may feed to the spreadsheet through automated links to other electronic sources or systems, or be keyed manually. Sources should be stated to enable figures to be checked.

> **Ian Wilson:**
> This figure represents total monthly sales per the Sage Invoicing system. It's uploaded to the sheet via Excel's link to Sage Line 50.

This example shows how the source may be explained using Excel's cell comment feature (which is explained later in this chapter).

Calculation methods

The calculation methods used should be stated, perhaps as a note or comment next to the calculation.

This is particularly important if complex calculation methods are used, or if regulations dictate a specific method should be used (eg depreciation methods for different classifications of assets).

Functions

The variables used in functions may require explanation to ensure the basis of the calculation is understood.

Spreadsheet packages such as Excel contain built-in functions. These are routines that may be used within a formula to perform particular tasks. For example, the function AVERAGE may be used to calculate the average value of a specified range of cells.

With some functions, the variables may require explanation. For example, the SLN function calculates the straight-line depreciation of an asset for one period. It uses the notation =SLN(cost,salvage,life)

If a spreadsheet includes the SLN function, the basis of the *life* variable should be explained (eg to calculate annual depreciation *life* would be stated in years (eg 3), to calculate monthly depreciation, *life* would be stated in months (eg 36).

Formatting

The nature and variety of formatting used should be documented, particularly if a range of formats are used or if there is any potential for confusion.

Formatting should be used to ensure the spreadsheet is clear, easy to read and understandable. Bold, italic, colour, shading and borders can all be applied to improve presentation and aid understanding. Try to achieve a clear, relatively simple look. When using colour, remember that some users may print the spreadsheet in black and white which may not clearly distinguish the colours used.

Values should be formatted appropriately and consistently. As a general rule, numbers should be right justified. Apart from titles and headings, text generally reads best if left justified. Column headers should be justified to match the numbers below.

Date formats can cause confusion, particularly if a spreadsheet is used in other countries (eg USA). To avoid confusion, use formats that specify letters for month names and four digits for the year (eg '10-Aug-2008' and 'Aug-2008' are unambiguous, but '10-08-08' and '08/08' are not).

When aligning a heading across a range of cells, don't merge the cells as this causes problems with copying and pasting ranges. Instead, use Excel's *Center Across Selection* alignment option (*Format > Cells*, *Alignment* tab, tick *Center Across Selection*).

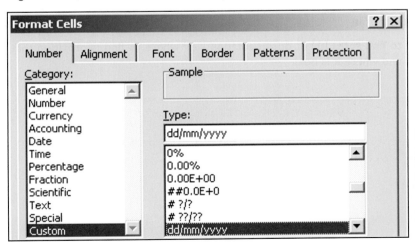

Excel offers a range of date formats in *Format > Cells*, *Number* tab, *Date* category. You can also specify your own formats (eg dd-mmm-yyyy) by selecting *Custom*.

User guidance

> Clear guidance should be provided to enable the spreadsheet to be updated and understood.

The more complex the spreadsheet, the greater the need for formal, detailed documentation. For example, a complex spreadsheet model that includes macros and visual basic programming is, in effect, a significant systems development project requiring formal systems development controls and documentation.

A summary or index worksheet may be used to provide guidance relating to spreadsheet navigation, organisation and structure.

If a significant amount of user guidance is appropriate, this may best be grouped together in a user manual.

Organising content

> Content should be arranged coherently using a clear and logical worksheet scheme.

Spreadsheet content should be organised in a manner that aids usability and understanding. How best to lay out content will depend upon the purpose of the spreadsheet and the nature and volume of data.

The way content is arranged (both within individual worksheets and across multiple sheets) should be considered and planned. As a general rule, worksheets that will be used as a calculation tool should ideally be constructed in three sections.

1. An inputs section containing the variables (eg for a loan the amount, term and interest rate).
2. A calculations section containing formulas.
3. The results section, showing the outcome the calculations.

Where should spreadsheet documentation be held?

There are a number of places where information relating to the spreadsheet could be held. Four possibilities are:

- ▶ Within the spreadsheet file properties
- ▶ As a comment or description within the spreadsheet
- ▶ In a documentation worksheet within the spreadsheet file
- ▶ In a separate document file

Users should know where to find spreadsheet documentation - or where to find information that details what documentation exists and where it is held.

Using the file properties

> The file properties provide a convenient place to store basic data relevant to the spreadsheet.

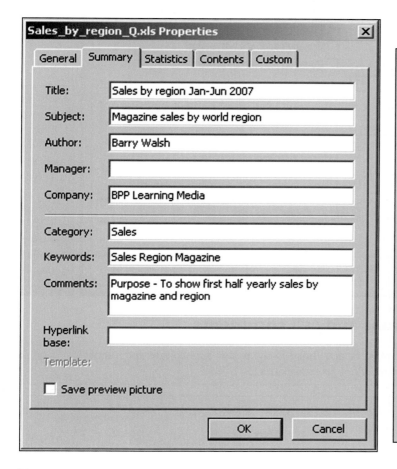

To access file properties in Excel 2003, open the spreadsheet and then select *File* > *Properties* from the Excel menu.

Entering data in the *Title*, *Subject*, *Author*, *Category*, *Keywords* and *Comments* fields provides easily accessible, basic data about the spreadsheet.

Author initially defaults to the registered user name of the software, but this may be changed. The *Comments* field provides one possible location to record the spreadsheet purpose.

Entering *Keywords* helps if the need arises to search for the spreadsheet (covered below).

Depending upon the version of Excel used, file properties may include other fields such as *Manager* and *Company*.

To search using *Keywords*, from within Excel select *File* > *File Search*. Select the *Advanced File Search* option, and from the *Property* box drop-down menu click *Keywords*. Change the *Condition* option to 'includes', then enter the word(s) you wish to search for in the *Value* field. Click *Go* to perform the search.

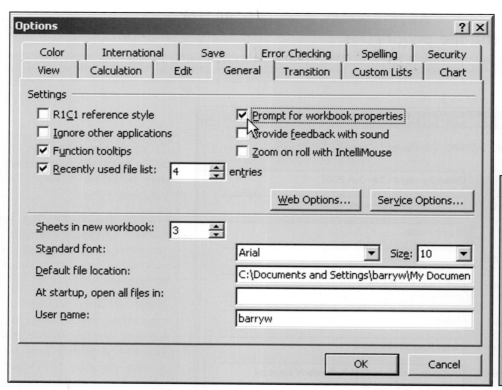

Excel includes an option to prompt for an update of the file properties each time the file is saved.

The *Prompt for workbook properties* option is available by selecting *Tools* > *Options* and activating the *General* tab.

Using text descriptions and cell comments

Text descriptions and cell comments are most likely to be appropriate for recording data sources, spreadsheet assumptions and instructions or explanations.

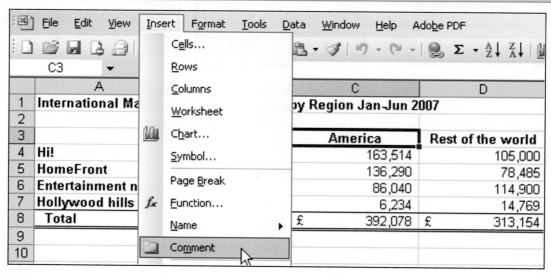

In the spreadsheet shown above, an appropriate comment in cell C3 could be 'Includes Canada, USA, Central and South America'. To attach a comment to a cell in Excel 2003, click the cell you want the comment attached to then select *Insert* > *Comment* from the Excel menu. When you've finished, simply click outside the box.

How comments or comment indicators are displayed on-screen depends upon the settings within the *View* tab (*Tools* > *Options* > *View*).

How comments are printed depends upon the settings within *File* > *Page Setup* > *Sheet* tab – in the *Comments* option.

Using documentation worksheets

General information and notes intended to help the user utilise the spreadsheet should be held within the spreadsheet workbook in a separate, suitably named worksheet.

This type of general information and notes are likely to be more substantial and detailed than that held to record basic facts (such as *Author*). This information may be best held in a separate worksheet (eg a worksheet named 'Instructions' or 'Explanatory notes').

41	Data:	Ensure the sales figure upload from the SOP system has been processed. Check with the head of sales ledger.
43	Commission rates:	Refer to the cell notes in the assumptions section of the Commission calculation sheet.
45	Payments:	No commission payments to be processed without sign-off by the Sales Director.

Commission calculation ╱ Source data ╲ **Instructions** ╱

Using separate documentation files

Larger, more complex spreadsheets require more extensive documentation. This is best held in separate document files.

As previously mentioned, complex spreadsheets require more formal, detailed documentation. This may best be held in a user manual.

One danger is that documentation held separately is forgotten or ignored. A separate note should be held within the spreadsheet workbook that gives the documentation location - and emphasises the importance of referring to it.

Backup routine

What is a backup?

A backup is a duplicate copy of a correct, usable file. The backup is stored separately and is used if the original file is lost or fails.

All organisations should have an effective daily backup routine that backs up all files held on their systems. Spreadsheet users should ensure their files are included as part of this routine, and that the files are restorable.

Network backups held onsite should be stored in a fireproof safe. To provide protection in case of a major disaster, the backup routine should specify which backups should be stored off-site (eg weekly).

Even with an effective daily backup routine, some work may be lost. For example, if after two hours work on a Wednesday a spreadsheet file becomes corrupt, restoring the back-up copy from Tuesday would still mean Wednesday's work is lost.

Users should consider making a separate backup copy - particularly if making changes to formulas or to the structure of the sheet. This could be copied to a separate network or hard-disk location, or to a different medium such as a memory stick, or a recordable CD.

Saving automatically

As an additional protection, the *AutoRecover* option within Excel can be set-up to automatically save a spreadsheet at specified intervals.

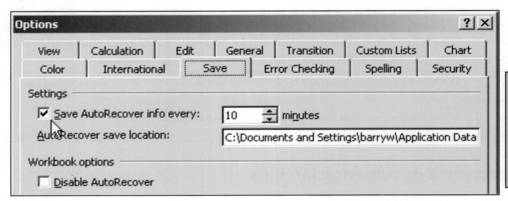

The settings for *AutoRecover* are accessed through *Tools > Options* and then selecting the *Save* tab.

Using Save <u>A</u>s or Open as <u>C</u>opy

One relatively common way spreadsheet information is 'lost' is by over-writing the original, 'complete' file with an incomplete or even a different file - by mistakenly saving the later file with the name of the original.

One way to reduce the chance of this happening is to save the original file with a different name or to a different location (using *File* > *Save <u>A</u>s*). This creates a copy to be worked on, leaving the original file intact.

The same can be achieved through opening the file as a copy of the original (using *File* > *<u>O</u>pen*, selecting the file and then choosing the *Open as <u>C</u>opy* option from the menu accessed via the down arrow on the *<u>O</u>pen* button).

Using this option with a file named Commission.xls would open a separate file named Copy (1) of Commission.xls.

Password protection

Password protection may be applied to spreadsheet files to prevent access and/or to prevent or restrict changes.

Attaching a password to a spreadsheet file

The most effective way of controlling access to information held in an Excel spreadsheet is to allocate a password to the file.

To assign a password to a spreadsheet file, open it, then from the *File* menu, select *Save As*. Next, click the *Tools* drop down menu and select *General Options*. A new dialogue box will appear as shown below.

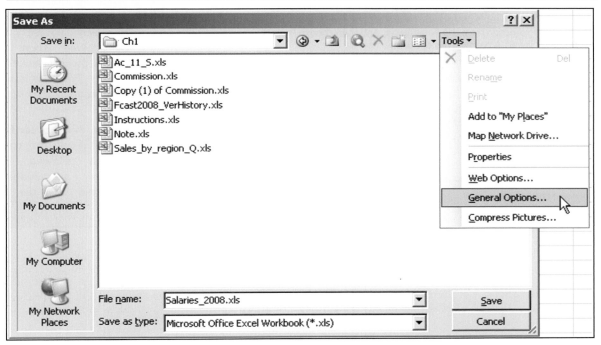

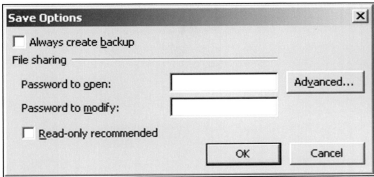

Type the password(s) you wish to assign to *open* and/or *modify* the document (or both), and click *OK*. You'll be asked to confirm the password(s) when the Save completes.

Applying password protection to worksheets

An individual worksheet can be protected, for example so users are only able to change or enter data in certain cells. Worksheet protection is often applied to prevent unauthorised and/or unintended changes to formulas within the sheet.

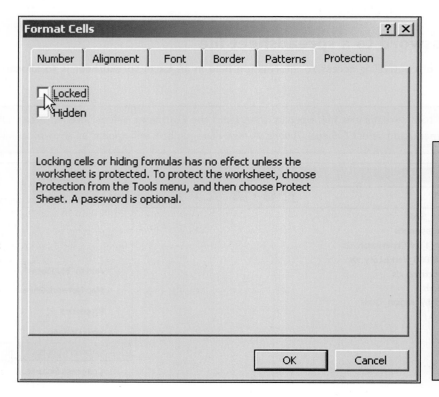

To apply this protection, start by selecting the cells to which data entry **is** to be allowed. Then, from Excel's menu select *Format > Cells*, *Protection* tab and clear (un-tick) the *Locked* box.

Repeat this process for all ranges of cells that entry is to be allowed. Then activate protection, as explained on the next page.

After specifying the cells into which data entry will be allowed, the next step is to activate protection of the sheet. This will protect all cells, except for those that have been specified for exclusion.

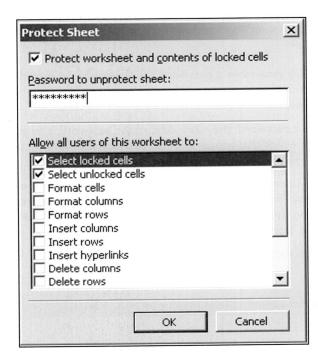

To activate protection, select *Tools* > *Protection* > *Protect Sheet*. Enter the password.

To clear the protection select *Tools* > *Protection* > *Unprotect Sheet* and enter the password.

Protecting workbook structure

Under the *Tools* > *Protection* menu option, Excel includes a *Protect Workbook* option. Activating this protection will prevent changes being made to the names and number of sheets in the workbook. This option does not provide any protection against changes to the content of worksheets.

Password format

Spreadsheet file (ie workbook passwords) provide more effective protection than worksheet passwords. To be effective against guesses and hacker tools, spreadsheet file passwords should contain at least 8 characters and include upper and lower case letters, numbers and non-alphanumeric characters (eg +, *, @, !, &).

There is a trade-off between being able to readily remember a password and the password providing the protection required. For example, using your name as a password would make it easy for you to remember but also easy for someone else to guess.

The more characters and types of characters in a password, the more difficult the password is to guess or to crack using an automated hacking tool. Using words that appear in a standard dictionary are particularly vulnerable to password guessing tools.

To create difficult-to-break but relatively easy-to-remember passwords, start by thinking of an event, a song, a film or anything that's memorable to you. For example, a Liverpool Football Club supporter may start by deciding their password will be based on the song 'You'll never walk alone'. This could be initially be shortened to WalkAlone (9 characters, mixed case).

Then to finalise the password, numbers and non-alphanumeric characters could be substituted for 'similar' letters, resulting in the password W@1kA10ne.

Password character substitution suggestions									
Letter	A	B	E	g	I	O	S	T	Z
Number	4	8	3	9	1	0	5	7	2
Symbol	@	&			!		$	+	?

Spreadsheet passwords should be changed at regular intervals, and should be changed earlier than scheduled if the password may have been compromised.

Password register

A record of spreadsheet passwords should be maintained in a secure location. Access to this must be controlled.

Macro security

Why is macro security important?

A macro is a script used to automate an action or a set of actions. Macros are recorded in the Visual Basic for Applications (VBA) programming language and may be used to automate actions within Excel. Unfortunately, some individuals produce malicious macros (macro viruses) intended to damage a system.

Setting the security level

Macro security level should be set at an appropriate level. An appropriate level is one that allows valid macros to be run, but blocks malicious macros.

Within Excel, security settings exist to provide protection against macro viruses. There is a trade-off between convenience and practical considerations, and the need for security. Applying a very high level of security is likely to prevent legitimate macros being utilised.

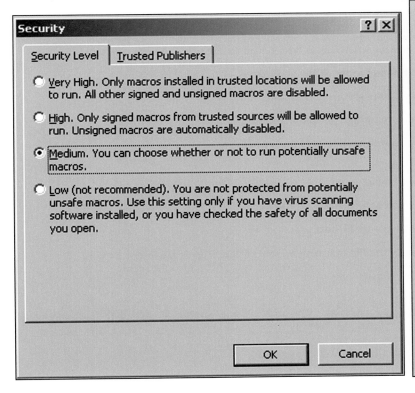

The macro security setting is accessed via _Tools_ > _Macros_ > _Security Level_. Four levels are available.

Very High only permits the running of macros from trusted sources and locations.

High only permits the running of macros from trusted sources (a less stringent check than _Very High_ as location is not included). Trusted sources may be amended in the _Trusted Publishers_ tab.

The _Medium_ setting instructs Excel to inspect macros for unsafe code before running. This is usually adequate but not 100% failsafe, as Excel may not detect unsafe code.

Selecting _Low_ indicates you're happy to rely on other checks to identify malicious macros.

To be recognised as originating from a macro publisher on the _Trusted_ list, the macro must be digitally signed by the publisher.

Regardless of the level of protection selected here, separate firewall and anti-virus software should be installed and maintained to detect and remove macro viruses.

Quick Quiz

Answer the following questions

1   When talking about spreadsheet development, the terms 'version' and 'release' are interchangeable as they mean the same thing.

    Is the above statement TRUE or FALSE?

2   Why would 'keywords' be entered within the file properties of a spreadsheet?

    A   To help with file searches

    B   To document the spreadsheet purpose

    C   To help the user understand the spreadsheet

    D   To record the name of the spreadsheet author

3   Which one of the following situations is best suited to the use of a cell comment?

    A   When the text needs to be visible at all times

    B   Holding detailed instructions and explanation

    C   Recording the spreadsheet author name

    D   Recording the source of data held in a cell

4   The main purpose of a backup is to:

    A   Enable another person to work on the file

    B   Ensure compliance with IT best practice

    C   Provide a copy of the file that may be used if the original file is lost or fails

    D   Ensure no work is ever lost

5   Which of the following passwords conforms to the password approach recommended under Spreadsheet Safe?

    A   proT3ction

    B   Spr3@dSh33+

    C   Wem8!ey

    D   All of the above

Answers to Quick Quiz

1   FALSE. 'Version' and 'release' do not mean the same thing. A version is a particular state or design of the spreadsheet. A release is a version that has been issued to users.

2   A. The main function of keywords is to help ensure relevant searches locate the file.

3   D. The other options are more suited to other locations (eg the file properties for C, a separate documentation file for B and a visible text description for A).

4   C. The main purpose of a backup is to provide a copy of the file that may be used if the original file is lost or fails.

5   B. This is the only password that contains at least 8 characters and includes all of upper and lower case letters, numbers and non-alphanumeric characters.

2 INPUT CONTROLS

Measuring points

▸ Place a single instance of a given constant (eg conversion or tax rates) in separate cells.
▸ Break down more complex formulas into smaller component parts to help with readability and comprehension, and for ease of update.
▸ Apply named ranges to make formulas more manageable.
▸ Use manual and automatic calculation modes.
▸ Make units of measure explicit.
▸ Apply the 'precision as displayed' setting.
▸ Import fixed length or delimited text files (eg CSV) into a spreadsheet and validate that the data types are correct.
▸ Reconcile the integrity of data from external sources as complete, consistent and correct.

SPREADSHEET SAFE™

| Setup | **Input controls** | Calculate | Output | Audit |

Constants

What is a constant?

In the context of spreadsheet design, a constant is a value, rate or factor used in one or more formulas or calculations. Examples include tax rates and exchange rates.

Using constants

> Constants should be distinguished (stored) separately, rather than being embedded within formulas.

Distinguishing a constant, by putting it in its own cell, facilitates the easy updating of the spreadsheet if the value of the constant does change.

If the constant does change, the spreadsheet can be updated by entering the new value in one cell, rather than needing to amend all formulas that use the constant. In the example shown below, cells D9:H9 all use the tax rate held in B5.

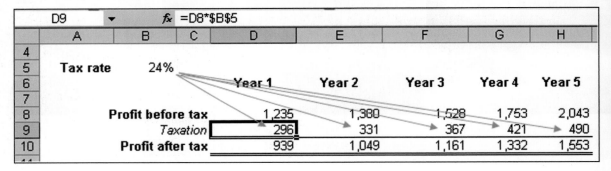

Named ranges

What is a range?

A range is an area of one or more cells. For example the 'Profit after tax' figures in the example above are held in the range D10:H10.

Using named ranges

> Range names should be used to simplify formulas.

Ranges can be named, to provide a user friendly way of referring to that area of the spreadsheet. The use of range names aids understanding in spreadsheet design and use.

In the example above, the cell B5 could be named 'TAX_RATE'. If this range name was created and then applied, the formulas in cells D9:H9 would use 'TAX_RATE' rather than $B$5.

Range names also help improve reliability. If changes are made to the structure of the spreadsheet that change the range references, the sheet can be updated quickly and accurately by changing the range name definition (if required - in many circumstances Excel is 'clever' enough to adjust the range references although these should be checked).

Creating a range name

Two ways to create a range name are explained below.

Option 1

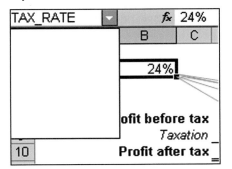

Select the cells you wish to name. This could be a single cell (eg B5), a number of adjacent cells or a number of non-adjacent cells.

Click the arrow head to the right of the Name Box (found to the left of the formula bar).

Type in the range name (eg TAX_RATE).

Option 2

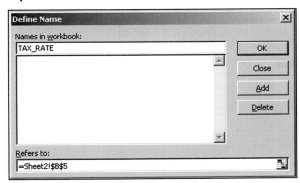

Select the cells you wish to name.

From the Excel menu, select *Insert* > *Name* > *Define*.

This displays the *Define Name* window.

Enter the range name in the *Names in workbook:* box.

Deleting or editing an existing range name

To delete an existing range name, use the *Delete* option available in the *Define Name* window (*Insert* > *Name* > *Define*). Existing ranges may be edited here too, by changing the references within the *Refers to:* field.

Displaying the *Define Name* box also provides a way of examining all existing defined named ranges.

Applying a range name

After a range is named, Excel does **not** automatically update formulas with the range name. To apply the range name to relevant formulas, follow these steps.

> Select all cells that include formulas that refer to the range (in the example below D9:H9). From the menu select _Insert_ > _Name_ > _Apply_.
>
> In the _Apply Names_ window, select the range name you wish to apply (this will already be selected if only one range name has been created). Leave the two checkboxes at the bottom of this window selected, then click OK.

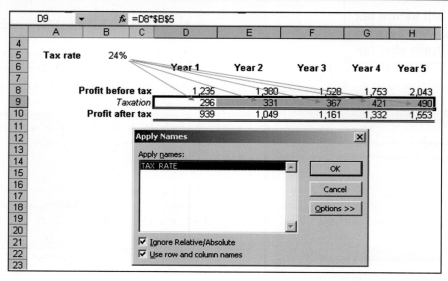

If you then examine the formulas in the cells selected, the range name (eg TAX_RATE) will be used instead of the cell range to which the name applies (eg $B$5).

Units of measure and conversion calculations

Why are 'units of measure' important?

All values within a spreadsheet relate to a unit of measure. To interpret figures correctly, users need to understand the unit of measure in which the figures are expressed.

Possible units of measure include:

- Currency (eg pounds, euros)
- A modified currency unit (eg £000s)
- A period of time (eg days)
- A date or specific point in time (eg day, month, year)
- Temperature (eg Celsius, Fahrenheit)
- Distance (eg centimetre, metre, yard, kilometre)
- Weight (eg gram, kilogram, ounce, pound)

Values may also be expressed as percentages, ratios or fractions.

Identifying and converting units of measure

> Units of measure used should be stated clearly and applied consistently. If conversion calculations are required, the conversion factors should be distinguished (stored) separately, rather than being embedded within formulas.

To avoid confusion, units of measure must be stated clearly and explicitly. Failure to do so is likely to hinder understanding and may lead to errors in spreadsheet logic - for example the lack of clarity may lead to formulas being constructed that 'add apples to oranges'.

3	Total sales	2,793
4	Total number of transactions	15,872
5	Average value per transaction	0.18

The sales figure here was entered without specifying the unit of measure. This has led to an incorrect average value calculation.

3	Total sales (£000)	2,793
4	Total number of transactions	15,872
5	Average value per transaction	£176

In this example, the unit of measure for sales was identified as £000. This allowed a correct average transaction value to be calculated.

Note the use of formatting to help clarity. In the lower example, the average transaction value figure has been formatted to display in pounds (ie without pence). As an additional guide, the number has been formatted to include the £ sign.

Conversion calculations

If a spreadsheet includes values that are to be converted from one unit of measure to another (eg pounds sterling to euros), the conversion factors should be distinguished (stored) separately, rather than being embedded within formulas.

This is achieved in the same way as explained (using the tax rate example) earlier in this chapter.

Manual and automatic calculation modes

Using the 'manual calculation' setting

> If *Manual* calculation is selected, recalculation of formulas is delayed until the user triggers a recalculation by pushing the F9 key.

Excel may be run in one of two main calculation modes; *Manual* or *Automatic* (the third mode, *Automatic except tables*, can cause confusion and should be avoided completely). This option is found under *Tools > Options*, in the Calculation tab.

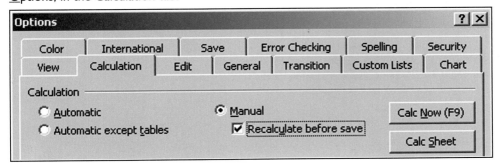

The setting applies to the Excel application, so it affects not only to the current file, but all spreadsheet files opened with that copy of Excel.

Under *Automatic* calculation, formulas recalculate immediately when new entries are made. However, when working on a particularly large or complex file, *Automatic* calculation may slow down the input process. After each new value is input, the spreadsheet will recalculate, which may delay the input of subsequent entries. Switching to *Manual* avoids this problem. Under *Manual* calculation, recalculation does not occur as new entries are made – it is delayed until the user triggers a recalculation by pushing the F9 key.

The use of *Manual* calculation was more common in the past, when personal computers had less processing power and the recalculation was therefore more likely to cause delays.

Using *Manual* calculation can cause confusion, as it is easy to forget values are not recalculating automatically. For example, a report may be printed showing totals that do not reflect other figures shown.

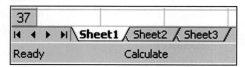

If calculation is set to *Manual* and a recalculation is required, the word 'Calculate' is displayed in the Excel status bar.

Even with this warning, there are many examples of embarrassing mistakes due to users switching to *Manual* recalculation but forgetting to force a recalculation.

Most users therefore prefer to use Excel with the calculation setting set to *Automatic*.

The *Precision as displayed* setting

What does the *Precision as displayed* setting do?

When Excel performs a calculation it uses the value stored in a referenced cell. The value stored is not necessarily the same as the value displayed. For example, if the value 1.055 is entered into a cell formatted to two decimal places Excel will display 1.06. Although 1.06 is displayed, the 'actual' value, 1.055, is used in calculations.

However, if the *Precision as displayed* setting is selected, all values are changed to match those displayed. In our example, the stored value 1.055 would be overwritten with the displayed value 1.06.

The advantage of using *Precision as displayed* is it prevents the appearance of confusing (although correct) calculation results. The disadvantage is that accurate values are overwritten with less accurate data, as demonstrated in the example that follows.

Using _Precision as displayed_

The _Precision as displayed_ setting may be used to overwrite values stored with values displayed. The values displayed will then be identical to the values used in calculations.

The example below demonstrates the effect of _Precision as displayed_.

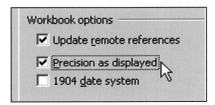

The value 100.5 is entered in cells A2, A3 and A4. These cells are formatted to display without decimal places, so Excel displays 101 in these cells.

Cell A5 contains the formula =SUM(A2:A4). This adds 100.5+100.5+100.5, resulting in a total of 301.5. As cell A5 is formatted to display without decimal places, Excel displays 301.5 as 302.

This could cause confusion, as a user viewing a hard copy of this data sees 101+101+101=302.

To apply the _Precision as displayed_ setting, select _Tools_ > _Options_ and then the _Calculation_ tab.

Click the _Precision as displayed_ box, then click _OK_.

Excel then warns you that _Data will permanently lose accuracy_.

To proceed (ie to overwrite stored values with displayed values), click _OK_.

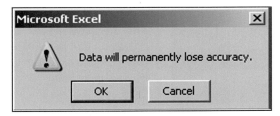

After applying _Precision as displayed_, the values held in cells A2, A3 and A4 are changed from 100.5 to 101.

Cell A5 contains the formula =SUM(A2:A4). The answer has changed though, as the formula is now adding 101+101+101, giving an answer of 303.

Although using _Precision as displayed_ can reduce confusion, it does so at the expense of accuracy. In the example above, 100.5+100.5+100.5=301.5. Therefore, displayed without decimal places, the first answer obtained is correct (302). The result obtained after applying _Precision as displayed_ (303) looks correct, but is incorrect based on the actual values originally input.

Precision as displayed is a workbook setting. It applies to all worksheets in a workbook, but does not affect other Excel files.

Importing data

Performing the import

Excel's *Text Import Wizard* facilitates the efficient input of data held in text files. Checks must be carried out to ensure data has imported correctly.

Excel includes a data import facility to allow efficient input of data held in text files (eg data exported to a text file from other applications).

To import data, using the Excel menu select *Data* > *Import External Data* > *Import Data*. In the *Files of type* box, click *All Files (*.*)*. Use the *Look in* drop down box to navigate to, and select, the file to be imported, then click *Open*. The *Text Import Wizard* will appear.

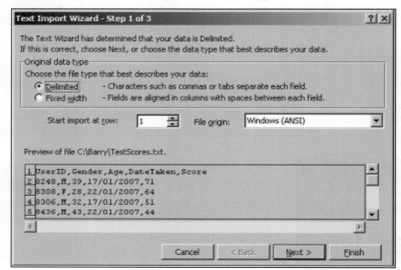

The *Text Import Wizard* defaults to the file type Excel has identified as best fitting the file to be imported. *Delimited* means the import file includes a character that separates pieces or fields of data.

The file used in this example contains comma-delimited data (the commas are visible in the *Preview of file* area).

Click *Next*.

The Wizard defaults to *Tab* as the delimiter. In our example, we would change this to *Comma*.

In the *Data preview*, lines have appeared showing how the data will be imported.

Click *Next*.

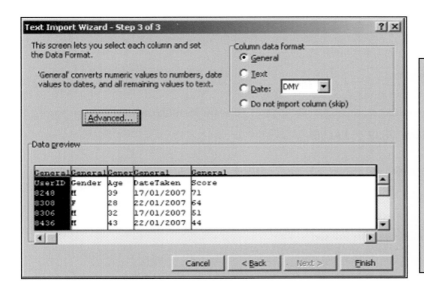

The Wizard then provides an opportunity to change the format of data in each column.

The *General* format is usually fine (this treats numeric values as numbers, date values as dates and everything else as text). If required, cells can be formatted appropriately within Excel, after the import is complete.

Click *Finish*.

You are then asked to indicate where the data should be imported to. Selecting the *New worksheet* option is safest as this ensures no existing data is overwritten by imported data.

Click *OK*, and your data will appear in the worksheet.

Validating the imported data

Checks should be performed to ensure data imported to Excel has imported correctly.

After the import, checks should be performed to ensure data held within Excel is as expected. The nature of the checks will depend upon the type of data imported.

Possible checks could include:

▸ Checking the number of records (rows), fields (columns) and populated cells (fields) in Excel against the source

▸ Sum numeric values in Excel and check the totals against totals from the source system

▸ Check all data has been imported (eg all expected columns and rows are present)

▸ Ensure dates are formatted correctly

Quick Quiz

Answer the following questions

I   After a range is named, Excel automatically updates relevant formulas with the range name.

     Is the above statement TRUE or FALSE?

2   In the context of spreadsheet design, what does the term 'unit of measure' refer to?

     A   Scales or factors used to measure and express quantity

     B   The file size, expressed in kilobytes (kb) or megabytes (Mb)

     C   The total number of cells utilised

     D   The number of cells dependant upon a specific cell

3   What does the word 'Calculate' signify in the illustration below?

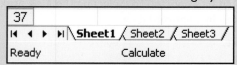

     A   The cursor is currently sitting in a cell that contains a formula

     B   Excel is currently running in *Manual calculation* mode and a recalculation update was the last action performed

     C   Excel is currently running in *Manual calculation* mode and a recalculation update is required

     D   Excel is currently running in *Automatic calculation* mode

4   If *Manual calculation* mode is selected, which key or keys should be pressed to trigger a recalculation?

     A   Ctrl and F9

     B   Shift and F9

     C   Alt and F9

     D   F9

5   Which of the following statements about the *Precision as displayed* setting is incorrect?

     A   Selecting *Precision as displayed* reduces accuracy

     B   Selecting *Precision as displayed* does not alter underlying values

     C   Selecting *Precision as displayed* can reduce the potential for confusion

     D   None of the above are incorrect

Answers to Quick Quiz

1   FALSE. After a range is named, the range name needs to be applied to cells containing relevant formulas.

2   A. The unit of measure is the scale or factor used to measure and express quantity. There are many possibilities, for example an item count (eg number of transactions), a currency (eg euros) or weight (eg kilograms).

3   C. 'Calculate' signifies that Excel is currently running in *Manual calculation* mode and a recalculation update is required.

4   D. If *Manual calculation* mode is selected, a recalculation is triggered by pressing F9.

5   B. Selecting *Precision as displayed* does alter underlying values.

Input controls ❖ Spreadsheet Safe

3 CALCULATE

Measuring points

▶ Use mathematical and logical formulas and functions in a spreadsheet.
▶ Correct the order of precedence of mathematical operators.
▶ Understand the concept of circular references in a spreadsheet. Recognise and remove circular references.
▶ Recognise array (matrix) formulas in spreadsheets.
▶ Check the number and type of function arguments (Lookup function).
▶ Check for and correct relative, absolute and mixed cell references.
▶ Create worksheet and spreadsheet links and validate that they summarise and update correctly, and are complete.
▶ Check for missing input values.
▶ Check for and correct missing precedent cells.
▶ Apply the ISERROR and ISNA functions.
▶ Correct #DIV/0! occurrences where appropriate.
▶ Check for and correct ####, #VALUE!, #NAME?, #REF and #NUM error values.
▶ Create cross-totals as a way to validate totalling.
▶ Check for and correct errors in totalling caused by row and/or column insertion or deletion.
▶ Check for and correct double counted sub-total errors.
▶ Check for and correct mismatched cross-total checks.
▶ Check for and correct automatic sum total errors.

SPREADSHEET SAFE™

| Setup | Input controls | **Calculate** | Output | Audit |

Formula construction

The Spreadsheet Safe task items focus on the checking and correcting of formulas (and functions). To check and correct formulas and functions you must first understand how to use and construct them.

This chapter includes some examples and explanations of formulas and functions. If you require further guidance, search Excel's *Help* (from Excel's main menu select *Help* > *Microsoft Excel Help*) for material relating to formulas (eg search for 'enter a formula') and functions (eg search for 'logical functions').

Order of precedence

To ensure formulae operate and calculate as intended, it's necessary to understand how Excel handles the order in which mathematical operations are carried out (the order of precedence).

'Order of precedence' refers to the sequence in which Excel performs mathematical operations. Excel calculates formulas using the order of precedence shown in the table below.

	Excel order of precedence for mathematical operators	
1	**:** - colon - single space **,** - comma	Reference operators
2	**-**	Negation (ie indicating a value is negative as in -1)
3	**%**	Percent
4	**^**	Exponentiation (ie the raising of a number to a given power)
5	***** and **/**	Multiplication and division
6	**+** and **-**	Addition and subtraction
7	**&**	The ampersand symbol used to connect strings of text (concatenation)
8	**= < > <= >= <>**	Comparison operators eg = equal to; > greater than; < less than; >= greater than or equal to; <= less than or equal to; <> not equal to sign

The order of precedence shown above **ignores the effect of brackets (parentheses)**.

The following points are also relevant when considering order of precedence.

▶ Calculations inside parentheses are performed first.

▶ Calculations are performed from left to right (eg if the formula contains more than one multiplication and/or division calculation, these are performed from the left).

▶ If the formula includes parentheses inside parentheses, the deepest nested parentheses are calculated first. From there, Excel works its way outwards.

Let's look at a simple example. Cell A1 contains 5, cell A2 contains 10 and cell A3 contains 20.

The formula =A1+A2*A3 would output 205. Excel would perform A2*A3 first (10x20=200), and then add 5 from cell A1.

Parenthesis may be used to change the order of precedence. The formula =(A1+A2)*A3 would first add A1 to A2, and would then multiply this result by A3. This would output 300 (as 5+10=15, and 15x20=300).

Similarly, the formula =A3-A2/A1 would give a result of 18. Excel would divide A2 (10) by A1 (5) and then subtract the result (2) from A3 (20).

=(A3-A2)/A1 gives a result of 2. Excel first subtracts A2 (10) from A3 (20) resulting in 10. This is then divided by A1 (which is 5), producing a result of 2.

Recognising array formulas

Array formulas display in the formula bar with braces (curly brackets), for example {=A1*A2}.

An array is a collection of items. In Excel, those items may reside in a single row or column, or multiple rows and columns. An array formula is a formula that can perform multiple calculations on one or more of the items in an array.

Array formulas can return either multiple results or a single result. They allow a single formula to be used instead of several different formulas.

Array formulas use standard formula syntax. To enter an array formula, instead of pressing *Enter* you press *Ctrl+Shift+Enter*. In the formula bar, Excel then surrounds the array formula with braces (curly brackets).

In the example below, the array formula in cell B6 multiplies the *Number of units* by the *Unit cost* for the three products, and adds the results together.

B6	▼	ƒx {=SUM(B2:D2*B3:D3)}		
	A	B	C	D
1		Product A	Product B	Product C
2	Number of units	100	50	50
3	Unit cost	1	3	2
4				
5				
6	Total cost	350		

Identifying and correcting errors

Removing circular references

Circular references usually (but not always) represent a mistake in the logic of the spreadsheet, for example a formula that includes a reference to its own cell address.

Here's an example of a circular reference error.

	A	B	
1			
2	Jan	2,100	
3	Feb	2,500	
4	Mar	2,600	
5	Quarter 1	=SUM(B2:B5)	

The formula held in cell B5 refers to cell B5 – a circular reference.

When a formula that contains a circular reference is entered, Excel displays the following warning.

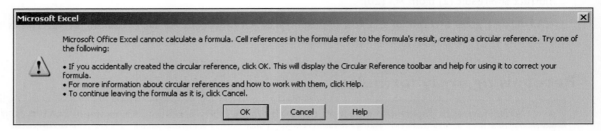

If this warning appears, Click *OK* to bring up the *Circular Reference* toolbar (shown below together with the meaning of the toolbar buttons).

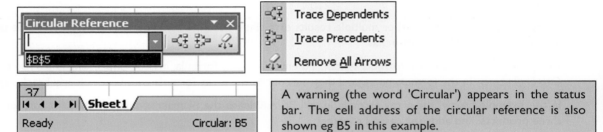

A warning (the word 'Circular') appears in the status bar. The cell address of the circular reference is also shown eg B5 in this example.

If 'Circular' appears without a cell reference, it means the workbook contains a circular reference but it isn't in the active worksheet.

Excel only provides one warning at a time, regardless of how many circular references are in the spreadsheet. When all circular references have been removed, the 'Circular' warning will disappear.

Checking for missing input values and precedents

Formulas should be checked for missing input values or precedents. Excel's formula auditing features can help with this process.

An 'input value' is a value entered into a cell. A 'precedent' is a cell referred to by the current cell.

Identifying missing input values is sometimes as simple as looking for empty cells within a range populated by values.

	A	B	C	D
1		**Revenue**	**Costs**	**Gross Profit**
2	North	2,543	890	1,653
3	South	5,487	1,920	3,567
4	East	2,855		2,855
5	West	3,642	1,275	2,367
6		14,527	4,085	10,442
7				

Cell C4 is missing an input value – the East region Costs.

This is also an example of a missing precedent, as C4 is referred to in formulas in D4 and C6.

In some situations, identifying missing input values requires an understanding of spreadsheet and calculation logic.

	A	B
1	**Student**	**Score**
2	Williams, S	56
3	Hatton, R	71
4	Barnes, J	47
5	Logan, G	
6	Ross, J	52
7	Weller, P	79
8		
9	Average	61

In this example, cell B5 is missing an input value.

The student G Logan did not sit the exam, so did not register a score. How this is recorded in cell B5 will effect the *Average* calculation in cell B9.

If cell B5 is left blank, the *Average* calculation will be based on five scores (even though six students are listed), giving an average of 61.

	A	B
1	**Student**	**Score**
2	Williams, S	56
3	Hatton, R	71
4	Barnes, J	47
5	Logan, G	0
6	Ross, J	52
7	Weller, P	79
8		
9	Average	51

If a score of zero is recorded in cell B5, the *Average* calculation will be based on six scores, giving an average of 51.

Using Trace precedents

	A	B	C	D
1		**Revenue**	**Costs**	**Gross Profit**
2	North	2,543	890	1,653
3	South	5,487	1,920	3,567
4	East	2,855	999	1,856
5	West	3,642	1,275	2,367
6		14,527	5,084	9,443
7				

To trace cells that provide data to a formula (precedents), click on the cell containing the formula, then from the menu select *Tools* > *Formula Auditing* > *Trace Precedents*. A tracer arrow then appears linking the active cell with precedent cells.

	A	B	C	D
1		**Revenue**	**Costs**	**Gross Profit**
2	North	2,543	890	1,653
3	South	5,487	1,920	3,567
4	East	2,855	999	1,856
5	West	3,642	1,275	2,367
6		14,527	5,084	9,443
7				

To identify the next level of precedents, remain in the active cell and select *Tools* > *Formula Auditing* > *Trace Precedents* again.

To remove the arrows, select *Tools* > *Formula Auditing* > *Remove All Arrows*. Rather than navigating through the menus, you may prefer to use the *Formula Auditing* toolbar. To display the toolbar, select *View* > *Toolbars* > *Formula Auditing*, or select *Tools* > *Formula Auditing* > *Show Formula Auditing Toolbar*.

Identifying and correcting error values

Errors should be identified, investigated and corrected. An understanding of Excel's error values is an important part of this process.

If Excel is unable to calculate a formula supplied it will return an error value. Common error values are explained in the table below.

Error value	Explanation
#DIV/0!	Commonly caused by a formula attempting to divide a number by zero (perhaps because the divisor cell is blank). The suppression and correction of #DIV/0! errors are covered later in this chapter.
#VALUE!	Occurs when a mathematical formula refers to a cell containing text, eg if cell A2 contains text the formula =A1+A2+A3 will return #VALUE!.
	Functions that operate on ranges (eg SUM) will not result in a #VALUE! error as they ignore text values.
	If the error results from a cell that appears to be blank, it's likely the cell holds one or more 'spaces' (ie entered by pressing the space bar). To clear the contents, use either the delete key - or select Edit > Clear > All (this option clears formats too).
	#VALUE! is a 'data type' error - we explain how to correct these later in this chapter.
#NAME?	The formula contains text that is not a valid cell address, range name or function name (for example a misspelt range name).
	Check the spelling of any functions used (eg by looking through functions under Insert > Function). To prevent the misspelling of named ranges use the Name Box to insert them into formulas.
	If the text is a range name that should exist, set the range up (define it). If the range name has been spelt incorrectly, correct the name in the formula.
	Check the syntax used in range references (eg correct use of colons, references to other worksheets contained in single quotes). Any text values entered in formulas should be enclosed in double quotation marks eg IF(B1=B2,"Match","No") .
#REF!	The formula includes an invalid cell reference, for example a reference to cells that have subsequently been deleted.
	If you notice the reference immediately after a deletion, use Edit > Undo Delete. Otherwise, investigation and editing of the formula to correct it is required. The Formula Auditing toolbar (View > Toolbars > Formula Auditing) may help with this process. The auditing toolbar and other options to help investigate errors may also be accessed by clicking on the error and then on the error button that appears ◇.
#NUM!	This error is caused by invalid numeric values being supplied to a worksheet formula or function. For example, using a negative number with the SQRT (square root) function.
	To investigate, check the formula and function logic and syntax. The auditing toolbar may help this process.
#N/A	A value is not available to a function or formula, for example omitting a required argument from a spreadsheet function. If data is not yet available, #N/A [or NA()] may be intentionally keyed into cells, so that formulas that refer to these cells also return #N/A rather than calculating a value. Again, the auditing toolbar may help the investigation process.

You should also be aware of the #### error. This is a display feature rather than an error value. It's usually caused by a column not being wide enough to display its contents. #### also occurs when a negative number is formatted as a date or time.

Using ISERROR and ISNA

ISERROR and ISNA are functions that may be used to prevent error values, for example if missing input values are expected.

D7	▼	*fx* =D5/D3		
	A	B	C	D
1				
2		Jan	Feb	Mar
3	Sales	20,000	25,000	
4	Cost of sales	12,000	14,000	
5	Gross profit	8,000	11,000	0
6				
7	Gross profit %	40%	◈%	#DIV/0!

> The formula in cell D7, =D5/D3, is correct, but as figures are not yet available for March, the formula returns the error value #DIV/0!
>
> This error value may cause confusion or concern to some recipients or users of the sheet.

D7	▼	*fx* =IF(ISERROR(D5/D3),0,D5/D3)		
	A	B	C	D
1				
2		Jan	Feb	Mar
3	Sales	20,000	25,000	
4	Cost of sales	12,000	14,000	
5	Gross profit	8,000	11,000	0
6				
7	Gross profit %	40%	44%	0%

> =IF(ISERROR(D5/D3),0,D5/D3) has been entered in cell D7. D5/D3 returns an error value (because figures for March have not been entered), but instead of the error value zero is displayed. When March figures are entered the result of the percentage calculation will be displayed.

ISNA may be used in an IF statement in the same way. The difference is that ISERROR returns TRUE for all error values, whereas ISNA returns TRUE for ~~all error values except~~ error values equal to #N/A.

ISERROR and ISNA should be used with care, to ensure errors that should be corrected aren't suppressed. You should also be aware of any possible 'knock-on' effect on other calculations of replacing the error value with zero (or with a text value such as a dash).

Using Conditional Formatting

Another approach is to not suppress the error value in the cell, but to hide it. This can be done using conditional formatting. A conditional format is a font, border or shading pattern that is applied if a specified condition is true.

In the example above, to hide the #DIV/0! error value in cell D7, select *Format* > *Conditional formatting*, set *Condition 1* to =ISERROR(D7), then click the *Format* button and choose the white as the font colour.

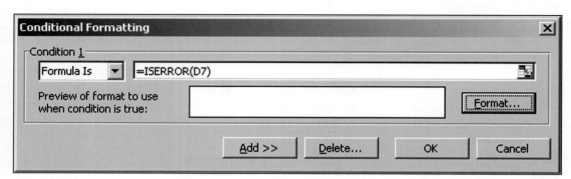

Relative, absolute and mixed cell references

Formulas should be checked to ensure relative, absolute and mixed cell references are used appropriately.

A relative cell reference in a formula changes if the formula is copied elsewhere. For example, let's say cell A3 contains the formula =SUM(A1:A2). If this formula was copied to B3, the formula in B3 would read =SUM(B1:B2). When using relative references, this formula means 'add the two cells above this one'.

An absolute cell reference in a formula does not change if the formula is copied elsewhere. For example, if =SUM($A$1:$A$2) was copied from cell A3 to cell B3, the formula in cell B3 would be identical – so would add A1 to A2.

A cell reference refers to a column (eg A) and a row (eg 3). In an absolute cell reference (eg $A$3), both the column and row items in the reference are absolute. Cell references may be mixed, that is they may combine absolute and relative items. In the reference $A3, only the column (A) is absolute. If A$3 is used, only the row (3) is absolute.

Finding and correcting cell reference errors

C41	▼		f_x =C40*B41	
	A	B	C	D
3			**Jan**	**Feb**
40	Profit before tax		4,905	5,175
41	Taxation	22%	1,079	5,584,343
42	Profit after tax		3,826	-5,579,168
43				

The formula in cell D41 is intended to calculate taxation at 22% on the Profit before tax. The result in D41 is obviously wrong, as it is greater than the profit.

C41	▼		f_x =C40*B41	
	A	B	C	D
3			**Jan**	**Feb**
40	Profit before tax		4905	5175
41	Taxation	0.22	=C40*B41	=D40*C41
42	Profit after tax		=C40-C41	=D40-D41
43				
44	**Formula Auditing** ▼ ×			
45	👁 🔓 🔒 ⬦ ⬦ 🔍 ◈ 🗐 🎽 🎽 📋 🔍			
46				

To investigate, first display formulas by selecting *Tools* > *Options* from the menu, and selecting the *Formulas* box on the *View* tab. This also brings up the *Formula Auditing* toolbar (or use *View* > *Toolbars* > *Formula Auditing*).

The formula in cell C41 refers to cell B41 using a relative address. It appears that this formula has been copied to D41, resulting in an incorrect calculation.

B41	▼		f_x 22%	
	A	B	C	D
3			**Jan**	**Feb**
40	Profit before tax		4905	5175
41	Taxation	0.22	=C40*B41	=D40*C41
42	Profit after tax		=C40-C41	=D40-D41

If we select B41 and then click the *Trace Dependents* button on the *Formula Auditing* toolbar, this confirms that only cell C41 is using the *Taxation* rate.

C41	▼		f_x =C40*$B41	
	A	B	C	D
3			**Jan**	**Feb**
40	Profit before tax		4,905	5,175
41	Taxation	22%	1,079	1,139
42	Profit after tax		3,826	4,037

The formula in C41 should have used $B41, so that when this was copied across the reference to column B was maintained.

After copying this formula, D41 calculates correctly.

Errors caused by row and column insertion or deletion

Formulas should be checked whenever changes are made to the spreadsheet structure. This is particularly important when rows or columns are inserted.

Generally, Excel automatically adjusts range references in formulas to reflect the deletion of rows and columns, including deletions made at the edge of the range. Dealing with the insertion of rows and columns requires more thought.

A common cause of error is the failure to update formulas after inserting rows or columns at the edge of an existing formula range. Generally, Excel formulas will adjust for insertions in the middle of a range, but may not update correctly for insertions at the edge of a range.

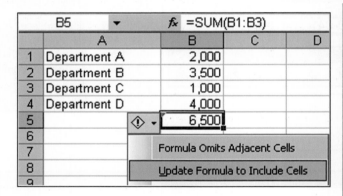

The formula in cell B4 is correct, =SUM(B1:B3).

A row has been inserted creating a new row 4 to which data has been entered. The formula is now held in cell B5, but remains as =SUM(B1:B3). The total is now incorrect as it excludes the data in the newly inserted row.

However, Excel does provide a screen tip warning. If from within this the *Update Formula to Include Cells* option is selected, this will correct the formula by extending it to include cell B4.

Always check any corrections made.

There is a setting within Excel that will adjust formulas for rows added at the end of a range, as in our example above. The *Extend data range formats and formulas* option is found under *Tools > Options*, in the *Edit* tab.

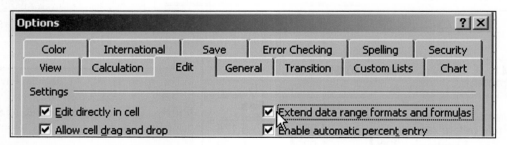

This is an application setting, so it applies to all workbooks opened after the setting is changed. To be extended, the formula must appear in at least three of the five rows preceding the new row.

Errors in sub-totals and grand totals

> Sub-totals and grand totals should be checked to ensure double counting and other types of error are avoided. Where appropriate, cross check totals should be used to validate calculations.

Double counted sub-totals

	A	B	C
1		**Sales 2007**	
2	North	2,543	
3	South	5,487	
4	Sub-total Region NS	8,030	← =SUM(B2:B3)
6	East	2,855	
7	West	3,642	
8	Sub-total Region EW	6,497	← =SUM(B6:B7)
10	Grand Total	29,054	← =SUM(B2:B8)

> Using SUM in B4, B8 and B10 (as shown) results in an incorrect Grand Total in cell B10.
>
> One approach to correct this would be to change the formula in B10 to add the two subtotal cells only, eg =SUM(B4,B8).

A more reliable approach to avoid double counting sub totals is the SUBTOTAL function. The syntax used is **SUBTOTAL(function_num,ref1,ref2,...)**.

The argument function_num specifies the function Excel should use with SUBTOTAL, eg the number 9 tells Excel to use SUM and to include values held in hidden rows, the number 109 tells Excel to use SUM but to ignore any values held in hidden rows.

	A	B	C
1		**Sales 2007**	
2	North	2,543	
3	South	5,487	
4	Sub-total Region NS	8,030	← =SUBTOTAL(9,B2:B3)
6	East	2,855	
7	West	3,642	
8	Sub-total Region EW	6,497	← =SUBTOTAL(9,B6:B7)
10	Grand Total	14,527	← =SUBTOTAL(9,B2:B8)

> Using SUBTOTAL in B4, B8 and B10 (as shown), results in the correct Grand Total in cell B10.

Differences in cross-check totals

Cross-check totals are created to validate other totals. A valid cross-check total provides added confidence that data included in column totals (added down) are included in row totals (added across).

F13	▼		f_x =IF(F10=F12,"OK","Cross-check difference")				
	A	**B**	**C**	**D**	**E**	**F**	
1	**Sales forecast**						
2		**2008**	**2009**	**2010**		**Total**	
3	*Sales*						
4	Shop 1	16,895	21,120	26,400		64,415	
5	Shop 2	9,870	12,340	15,425		37,635	
6	Shop 3	12,630	15,788	19,734		48,152	
7	Shop 4	4,900	6,125	7,656		18,681	
8	Online	17,650	22,063	27,578		67,291	
10	*Total Sales*	61,945	77,435	96,794		236,174	
12				Check		236,174	
13						OK	

The total in F10 is calculated =SUM(F4:F9)

To check or validate this, a cross-check total has been inserted in F12, =SUM(B10:D10)

An IF statement has been inserted in F13 to compare the two totals (refer to the formula bar shown in the screen image).

AutoSUM errors Σ ▾

Blank cells or cells with or non-numeric entries can cause problems when using Excel's *AutoSUM* button.

	A	B
1		**Sales 2007**
2	North	2,543
3	South	
4	East	2,855
5	West	3,642
6		=SUM(B4:B5)

Clicking in B6 and then clicking on the *AutoSUM* button results in Excel suggesting =SUM(B4:B5). Excel has assumed the range required ended at the blank cell B3.
To avoid this error, the range suggested by *AutoSUM* should always be checked, and if necessary edited, before it's accepted. In this case B4 should be changed to B2.

Validating the number and type of arguments in 'lookup' functions

Lookup functions such as VLOOKUP and HLOOKUP should be checked to ensure they operate as intended. The checking of function syntax and arguments is important in this context.

Excel includes a number of lookup functions. Lookup functions enable data held in a table to be examined and values identified.

VLOOKUP (ie vertical lookup) searches for a specified value from a vertical group of rows and then identifies a value from a specified column in that row. The syntax used (shown below) includes four arguments inside the brackets, each separated by a comma.

VLOOKUP(lookup_value,table_array,col_index_num,range_lookup)

	Argument	Explanation
1	lookup_value	The value to be found in the first column of the array (or the cell address of an additional input cell that contains the specified value).
2	table_array	The cell range or a range name containing the table of data.
3	col_index_num	The column number for the value you want returned.
4	range_lookup	TRUE or FALSE to specify whether to find an approximate match (use TRUE) or an exact match (use FALSE). If range_lookup is omitted, it's assumed to be TRUE, so an approximate match is returned. To reduce the potential for confusion, we recommend you always explicitly specify TRUE or FALSE (more likely).

D2	▼	*fx* =VLOOKUP(A2,A5:C8,3,FALSE)	
	A	B	C	D
1	**Enter student surname in the box below**			**Score**
2	Riley			54
3				
4	**Surname**	**First name**	**Score (%)**	
5	Williams	Tony	47	
6	Davies	Pippa	73	
7	Riley	Ola	54	
8	McAllister	Frank	68	

The formula in D2 (displayed) has correctly 'looked up' the score for the name entered in A2.

If "Rilley" (as opposed to "Riley") was entered in A2, the lookup would fail and cell D2 would return #N/A.

HLOOKUP (ie horizontal lookup) searches for a specified value from a horizontal group of columns and then identifies a value from a specified row in that column. The syntax uses the same logic as VLOOKUP, with the third argument referring to the row index number rather than a column.

HLOOKUP(lookup_value,table_range,row_index_num,range_lookup)

D2	▼	*fx* =HLOOKUP(A2,B4:E6,3,FALSE)		
	A	B	C	D	E
1	**Enter student surname in the box below**			**Score**	
2	Riley			54	
3					
4	**Surname**	Williams	Davies	Riley	McAllister
5	**First name**	Tony	Pippa	Ola	Frank
6	**Score (%)**	47	73	54	68

The formula in D2 (displayed) has correctly 'looked up' the score for the name entered in A2.

Note the row index in the formula is 3 (as 'Score' is the third row of data, rather than the actual row number.

Creating and maintaining links

Formulas that span more than one file require particular care to ensure the links are set up correctly and remain valid. Links may need to be modified to cope with changes relating to file names, location, workbook structure and worksheet structure.

During formula entry, links are best created by navigating to, and then selecting, the required range. As well as helping with accurate range identification, this also ensures the correct syntax is used. When linking to ranges in separate files (ie a separate workbook), ensure the file or files you wish to link to are open before starting to enter the formula.

Referring to a different worksheet in the same file

A reference to a range in a different worksheet (in the same file) displays the worksheet name with an exclamation mark. For example, if a formula in a sheet named *Summary* added the values in the range C10:C25 in a sheet named *Jan*, the reference would appear as **=SUM(Jan!C10:C25)**.

Referring to a different spreadsheet file

Links to external files display in two ways, depending on whether the source workbook is open or closed.

When the source file is open, the link displays the file name in square brackets, the worksheet name with an exclamation mark, and the range. The default format for references to ranges in other files is absolute references. Here's an example of a reference to an open file, **=SUM([Annual.xls]Jan!$C$10:$C$25)**.

When the source file is closed, the link also includes the path (the source file location). Single quotes are also added, one at the start of the path the other after the sheet name, eg **=SUM('C:\Sales\[Annual.xls]Jan'!$C$10:$C$25)**.

Maintaining links between files

As explained above, a formula that links to a range in a different spreadsheet file includes the source file location and file name. If the source file is closed, its location is displayed in the formula eg **=SUM('C:\Sales\[Annual.xls]Jan'!$C$10:$C$25)**

Changes to file name or location made in Excel

If linked workbook files are opened simultaneously in Excel and then saved using different names and/or locations, Excel will automatically update the links.

Changes to file name or location made outside Excel

If source file names or locations are changed outside Excel (or if files are deleted), the links within Excel aren't updated and will therefore be pointing to an incorrect location. If subsequently a different file is renamed to the original name and location, the links would be pointing at a different workbook.

Checking links

When links between files are established it's essential they are checked thoroughly. Use the techniques mentioned elsewhere in this book (eg range names, absolute cell references, formula auditing, cross-checks etc) to ensure links operate as intended.

The spreadsheet documentation should identify links and explain the logic behind them.

If changes are required to file names or location, these should be made with all relevant files open in Excel, so links are updated. Checks should be carried out after changes have been made to ensure the links operate as intended.

Quick Quiz

Answer the following questions

1   A formula is required to add the values held in cells B2 and B3, and then multiply the result by the value held in B4. Currently, the formula is incorrect =B2+B3*B4. What is the correct formula?

2   Which of the following symbols surrounds the contents of an array formula viewed in the formula bar?

    A   ( )
    B   [ ]
    C   { }
    D   # #

3   What does the word 'Circular' signify in the illustration below?

    A   There is only one circular reference in the active worksheet, in cell B5
    B   There is a circular reference in cell B5 of the active worksheet, and there may be others
    C   Cell B5 has been defined as a named range, 'Circular'
    D   A circular drawing object has been selected and the closest cell is B5

4   If the formula =SUM(A1:A3) is enteterd in cell A4 below, what will the formula return?

	A
1	100
2	300
3	Nil
4	

    A   #VALUE! - as the formula refers to a cell containing text
    B   #REF! - as A3 is an invalid cell address
    C   #NUM! - as 'Nil' represents an invalid numeric value
    D   400 - as SUM will ignore the text in A3

5   Which of the formulas shown below would look up 'Joanne' in column A, and return the associated value from column B?

	A	B
1	David	66
2	Joanne	59
3	Patrick	55
4	Vimal	71

    A   =VLOOKUP("JOANNE",A1:B4,2,FALSE)
    B   =VLOOKUP("Joanne",A1:A4,2,FALSE)
    C   =HLOOKUP("Joanne",A1:B4,2,FALSE)
    D   None of the above

Answers to Quick Quiz

1   =SUM(B2:B3)*B4 or =(B2+B3)*B4.

2   C. Array formulas display in the formula bar with braces (curly brackets), for example {=A1*A2}.

3   B. 'Circular' displays if the spreadsheet includes at least one circular reference. B5 represents the cell address of one circular reference. Excel only provides one warning at a time, regardless of how many circular references are in the spreadsheet. When all circular references have been removed, the 'Circular' warning will disappear.

4   D. =SUM(A1:A3) will return 400 as functions such as SUM that operate on ranges ignore text values. If A4 contained =A1+A2+A3, the specific reference to A3 would result in a #VALUE! error.

5   A. =VLOOKUP("JOANNE",A1:B4,2,FALSE) would find and return Joanne's score (in lookup functions text strings aren't case sensitive).

4 OUTPUT

Measuring points

▸ Show hidden data by changing custom formats (font or background colour), handling hidden zero values.
▸ Distinguish the format decimal command from the round function.
▸ Apply the format decimal command and the round function.
▸ Export data as CSV, tab delimited or other file format, and validate as correct.
▸ Print and proof spreadsheet output.
▸ Create a chart based on source data.
▸ Switch between different chart types.
▸ Change the orientation of a chart so that all data series are visible.
▸ Apply appropriate chart axes, orientation, scales, titles and annotation to enhance chart meaning.
▸ Express data in a chart meaningfully by choosing an appropriate chart type.

SPREADSHEET SAFE™

| Setup | Input controls | Calculate | **Output** | Audit |

Formats and settings

Show data hidden using formatting

A number of options and features within Excel may be used to hide spreadsheet content. This may be useful, for example for presentation purposes. However, suppressing or hiding content could potentially be used in an attempt to deceive.

Hidden zero values

The default setting in Excel is to display zero values. This can be changed, so cells that hold a zero value do not display it (ie a blank cell is displayed instead).

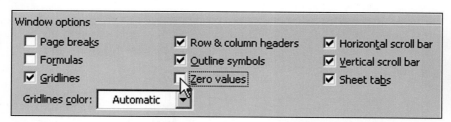

To suppress the display of zeros select *Tools* > *Options* then in the *View* tab remove the tick from the *Zero values* box.

To reveal zero values change the setting back to the default by 'ticking' the *Zero values* box.

Hidden cells

When a 'normal' cell is selected, the contents display in the formula bar. This display can be suppressed by formatting the cell as *Hidden*.

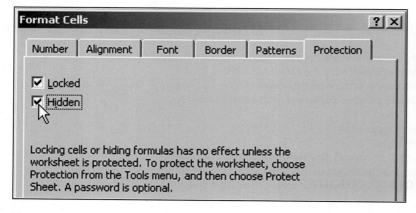

To prevent cell contents appearing in the formula bar, highlight the relevant cells, select *Format* > *Cells* and then in the *Protection* tab tick *Hidden*.

Cell contents will only be hidden if the sheet is protected (*Tools* > *Protection* > *Protect sheet*).

To reverse this setting, unprotect the sheet, select the relevant cells (or the entire worksheet if appropriate) and then remove the tick from the *Hidden* box.

Custom formats

Custom formatting options may be used to hide cell contents.

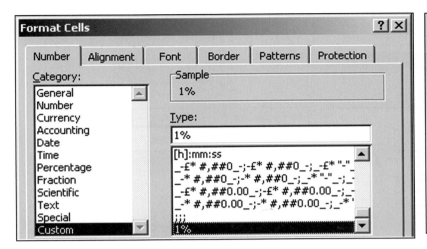

Custom formats may be accessed (and new formats set up) under *Format > Cells, Number tab, Custom Category*.

Applying a format 1% (shown), would result in 1% being displayed in a cell rather that the underlying value.

This could be used dishonestly, as shown in the example below.

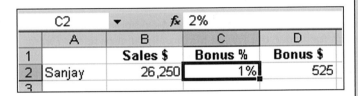

The custom format shown above has been applied to cell C2. However, the value in the cell is 2%, as shown in the formula bar.

Cell D3 contains the formula =B2*C2. The underlying value of 2% is used in the calculation.

The deception could be taken a step further by preventing the cell contents displaying in the formula bar using the H*i*dden cell format described in the previous section.

Another custom format to be aware of is the three semi-colon format ';;;' (shown above the 1% format in the *Format Cells* illustration). When applied, this displays a blank cell regardless of the cell contents.

To search for custom formats, scroll through the list under *Format > Cells, Number* tab, *Custom Category*, looking for suspicious entries. Further techniques to reveal data hidden using custom formats are explained later in the 'Revealing hidden data' section.

Font and background colour

If cells are formatted using the same colour for both the font and background, values are hidden from view. If selected, the cell contents will display in the formula bar, unless the cell is formatted as hidden and the worksheet is protected (as explained earlier in this chapter).

The techniques explained in the next section 'Revealing hidden data' will reveal content hidden in this way.

Revealing data: option I

To find cells formatted in a certain way, such as those formatted to suppress the display of data, from Excel's main menu select *Edit* > *Find*. In the *Find and Replace* window, click the *Options* button to reveal the options shown below.

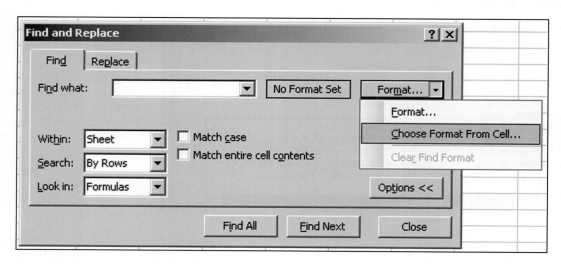

The window shown above enables you to search the current Sheet or Workbook for cells formatted in a certain way. Specify the format to search for under the *Format* button. If you choose the *Format* option, you're able to choose the options of the format you wish to search for. If you have already identified a cell formatted in a certain way and wish to find other cells that use the same format, select the *Choose Format From Cell* option.

Revealing data: option 2

This option will reveal worksheet content if the worksheet and workbook are protected (without *Hidden* formatting).

Select the contents of the entire worksheet (click on the corner of the top left corner of worksheet above the row 1 label and to the left of the column A label). Use your mouse to right click anywhere on the sheet, and from the pop-up menu select *Copy*.

Open a new workbook and select the 'contents' of an entire blank worksheet. Right click, and from the pop-up menu select *Paste Special*. Select the *Formulas* radio button and click *OK*.

All hidden content is revealed.

After following the steps above, clicking on a cell in the 'new' worksheet will result in the formula displaying in the formula bar as 'normal'.

To view all formulas, select *Tools* > *Options* and in the *View* tab 'tick' *Formulas*.

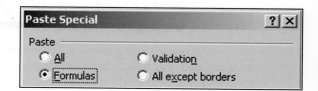

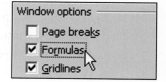

The difference between the ROUND function and formatting decimals

Excel's ROUND function works in a different way to the options available within Excel to format numbers. The ROUND function produces values that are different to those they are based on (it changes the underlying value).

Formatting numbers changes how values are displayed, without changing the underlying value.

	Sales	Share	ROUND and formatted	Formatted only
North	22,675	21.47%	21%	21%
South	34,240	32.43%	32%	32%
East	26,890	25.47%	25%	25%
West	21,785	20.63%	21%	21%
	105,590	100.00%	99%	100%

The **Share** column is =(Sales/Total Sales), formatted as a percentage to two decimal places.

The **ROUND and formatted** column uses =ROUND(Sales/Total Sales,2). The rounded values have been formatted to display zero decimal places (eg the rounded value 21.00% displays as 21%).

The **Formatted only** column is the same as **Share**, but formatted to zero decimal places (eg the value 21.47 is preserved but displays as 21%).

As shown in the example above, if a total is required, a more accurate total will be obtained if the values to be totalled are formatted rather than rounded. To ensure the accuracy of the total, the *Precision as displayed* setting (explained in Chapter 2) should remain 'off'.

Exporting data

Performing the export

Excel includes a number of converters that enables data to be exported in a range of formats such as Comma Separated Variable (CSV). Checks should be carried out to ensure data has exported correctly.

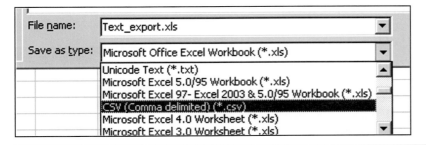

To export data from the active sheet, select *File* > *Save As* from Excel's main menu. Then choose an appropriate file type from the list available in the Save as type: box.

For example, if you wish to export data from Excel into an application that supports the import of Comma Separated Variable (CSV) files, choose the *CSV (Comma delimited)* format. Another common format is *Text (Tab delimited)*, which uses the '.txt' file extension.

If a dialog box is displayed, warning that the *Selected file type will only save active sheet*, click *OK*.

If a second box is displayed, asking if you wish to keep the workbook in the chosen format, click *Yes*.

Before you export

Check the data format required before performing the export, for example if the data will be imported into a different application ensure you're aware of the file format and structure that application requires.

What is exported?

If you export to a comma or tab delimited format, only the active sheet is exported. If your workbook has data on more than one sheet, each sheet should be exported individually. The exported file will include the cell contents as they were displayed in the spreadsheet.

Columns will be separated by commas (comma delimited files) or tabs (tab delimited files). Each row ends in a carriage return. If a cell contains a comma, the cell contents are enclosed in double quotation marks. If cells display formulas instead of formula values, the formulas will be exported as text.

What isn't exported?

Some features, such as formatting, will not be preserved in the exported data (Excel provides a warning about this during the export process). All formatting, graphics, objects, and other worksheet contents are lost. The euro symbol will be converted to a question mark.

Validating the exported data

Checks should be performed to ensure data has exported correctly.

After the exported file has been created, checks should be performed to ensure data has exported as expected. The nature of the checks will depend upon the type of data exported.

To conduct a general visual check, it's a good idea to close Excel and open the exported data in a different application, such as Notepad or WordPad (see examples below).

More detailed checks may be best done in Excel. For example, a check on the number of rows exported would be easier in Excel.

```
Text_export.csv - Notepad
File  Edit  Format  View  Help
UserID,Gender,Age,DateTaken,Score
8248,M,39,17/01/2007,71
8308,F,28,22/01/2007,64
8306,M,32,17/01/2007,51
8436,M,43,22/01/2007,44
8231,M,21,22/01/2007,52
```

An extract of a CSV file, viewed in Notepad.

```
Text_export.txt - Notepad
File  Edit  Format  View  Help
UserID   Gender   Age   DateTaken     Score
8248     M        39    17/01/2007    71
8308     F        28    22/01/2007    64
8306     M        32    17/01/2007    51
8436     M        43    22/01/2007    44
8231     M        21    22/01/2007    52
```

An extract of a tab delimited file, viewed in Notepad.

If data is subsequently imported into a different application, reports should be run from within that to verify data imported.

Printing and proofing

Spreadsheet output will often be printed. Printed output should be inspected before circulation to ensure it contains what was intended and presents information clearly.

The printing options available within Excel are extremely flexible. The material below includes some tips that may be applied to print spreadsheet content in such a way that aids communication and understanding. If you require further guidance, please refer to Excel's *Help* facility (eg search *Help* using 'printing').

Printing tips
Use print preview
Before you print, preview your worksheet. To open print preview, select *Print Preview* from the *File* menu, or click the *Print Preview* button on the standard toolbar.
Fit output on one page
To fit output to one page, select *File > Page Setup*, *Page* tab and under *Scaling*, click *Fit to 1 page(s) wide by 1 page(s) tall*. Avoid using this setting if as a result the output print size is too small to be read easily.
Fit output to a specific number of pages
To fit output to a specific number of pages, select *File > Page Setup*, *Page* tab and under *Scaling*, experiment with the *Fit to x page(s) wide by x page(s) tall* setting. Check the result using print preview.
Create or amend page breaks
On the *View* menu, click *Page Break Preview*. Drag the dotted blue line (the automatic page break) you wish to change to the desired location.
To reset an individual page break, drag the line to the left and off the print area. To reset all page breaks, right-click and then select *Reset All Page Breaks*.
Print part of a worksheet
To set a specific area as the print area, select the area then click *File > Print Area*, and then click *Set Print Area*. To clear the set print area select *File > Print Area > Clear Print Area*.
To print a selection as a 'one-off', select the area to be printed, then click *File > Print* and under *Print what* click *Selection*.
Print row and / or column headings on every page
From the *File* menu click *Page Setup*, in the *Sheet* tab enter details in the *Rows to repeat at top* and *Columns to repeat at left* boxes.
Prevent formula errors printing
From the *File* menu click *Page Setup* then in the *Sheet* tab under *Print* change the drop-down box option *Cell errors as:* to read *<blank>* or *- -* (whichever you prefer). Rather than using this option, it may be preferable to correct the error!
Add headers and /or footers
From the *File* menu click *Page Setup* and select the *Header/Footer* tab. Click the *Custom Header* or *Custom Footer* button, then either the *Left*, *Center* or *Right* section box. Experiment with the buttons (eg file name, date, page number etc).
Print formulas
From the *Tools* menu click *Formula Auditing* and then *Formula Auditing Mode*. Print the worksheet. To return to the formula results select *Tools > Formula Auditing > Formula Auditing Mode*.

Charts

Charts are a powerful visual tool. To communicate the underlying data in a meaningful way requires the selection of an appropriate chart type and settings.

Chart creation

The easiest way to produce a chart in Excel is to use the *Chart Wizard*. Although Excel can chart non-adjacent blocks of data, the *Chart Wizard* works most easily if the data to be included is in a single block with labels directly above and to the left of the data.

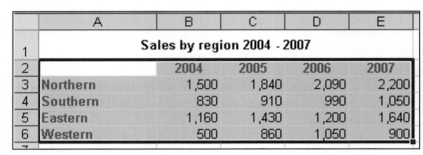

	A	B	C	D	E
1	Sales by region 2004 - 2007				
2		2004	2005	2006	2007
3	Northern	1,500	1,840	2,090	2,200
4	Southern	830	910	990	1,050
5	Eastern	1,160	1,430	1,200	1,640
6	Western	500	860	1,050	900

To create a chart, first select the data area, then click on the *Chart Wizard* button in the standard toolbar.

The *Wizard* takes you through four steps.

Step 1: Chart Type
We explain the chart type options in the following section.

Step 2: Chart Source Data
This includes the *Data Range* and *Data Series* options. If the source data has been arranged appropriately the Wizard should suggest the correct range and series.

Step 3: Chart Options
Includes *Titles, Axes, Gridlines, Legend, Data Labels* and *Data Table*. The chart title, legend and other labels should help convey what the chart is 'about'. Be careful not to clutter the chart with too many labels.

Step 4: Chart Location
Two options are available, *As new sheet:* and *As object in:*. The chart may be created in a new sheet by itself or as an object in the original worksheet (with the data).

Further information about the options most relevant to the Spreadsheet Safe task items is provided in the remainder of this section. If you require further general guidance relating to chart creation, detailed information is available in Excel's *Help* (search Excel *Help* using 'create chart').

Chart type

Charts should be formatted in a way that communicates information appropriately and effectively. An important part of this is choosing an appropriate chart type. Chart type is specified during initial chart construction. However, the chart type may easily be amended after set up. It may be appropriate to experiment and view a number of chart types before deciding which type best gets the message across.

To change the type of chart, right click in the chart area and from the pop-up menu select *Chart Type*.

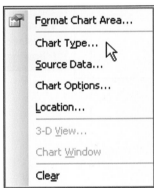

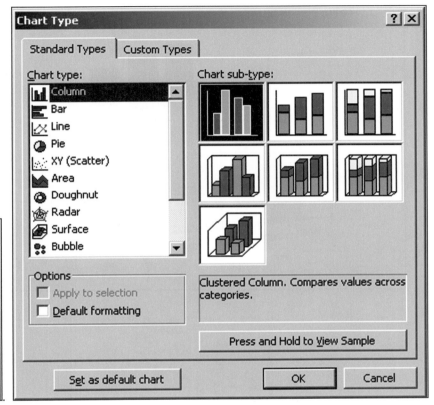

Choose the chart type you believe provides the clearest presentation of the relationship between the data series included. For example:

▸   If showing parts of a whole, a *Pie* chart may be most appropriate (eg analysing a single figure)

▸   For a cause-effect relationship, try an *XY (Scatter chart)* with trend lines

▸   A time-series may suit a *Column* or *Line* chart

▸   For multiple series, a *Staked column* (a choice within the *Column* type) may be appropriate

Data series

It's important that all data series are clearly visible and reflect the source data meaningfully.

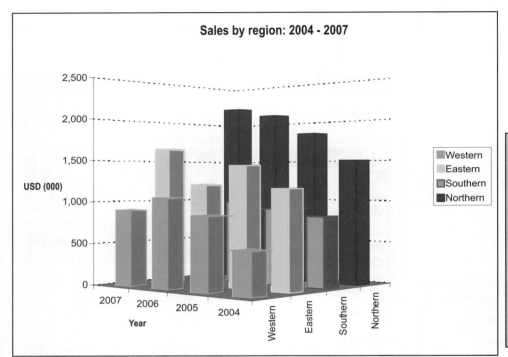

In this chart, som data series value are hidden (eg th 2005, 2006 an 2007 Souther values).

Visibility problem may be able to b fixed by changin the orientation o viewing angle (a explained on th following page).

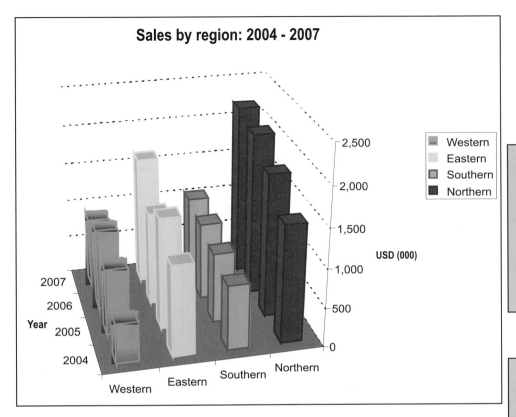

Sales by region: 2004 - 2007

Legend:
- Western
- Eastern
- Southern
- Northern

USD (000)

Axis values: 0, 500, 1,000, 1,500, 2,000, 2,500

Year: 2004, 2005, 2006, 2007

Regions: Western, Eastern, Southern, Northern

To change the orientation or angle of view, hold the mouse pointer over a corner of the chart - the pointer becomes a crosshair as shown below.

Use your mouse to drag the corner handle to rotate and tilt the chart until all values are visible.

One possible view is shown here.

Another approach to ensure data series are visible and display in a way that best conveys their meaning is to try a different chart type or sub-type. Sometimes a simple chart, such as the *Clustered Column* chart below, may communicate the message more clearly.

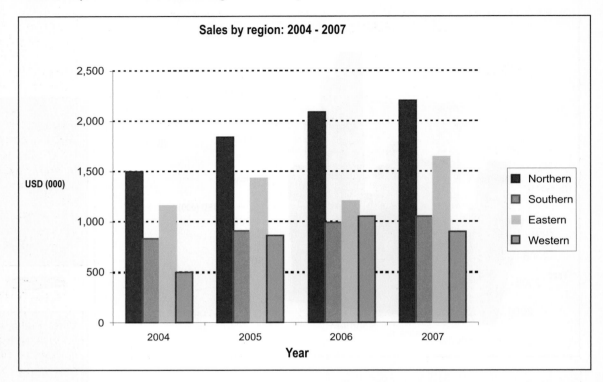

On the other hand, you may feel the *3D Column* chart on the previous page displays the values and trends more clearly.

Chart axes

The scale used on chart axes should enable the data series to display in a meaningful, fair way.

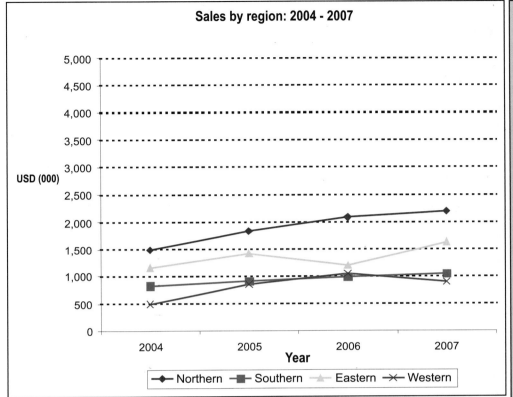

Sales by region: 2004 - 2007

The maximum value of 5000 on the y axis is far larger than the highest value (2,200).

As a result the sales trends on the graph appear relatively insignificant, which is misleading.

To adjust the scale, point to the relevant axis and double-click (or click once to select the axis, then right click and select *Format Axis*). You are then presented with the options shown on the following page.

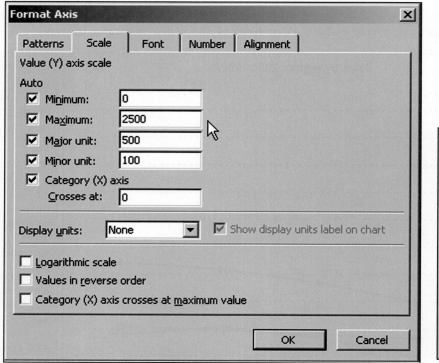

Format Axis

Patterns | Scale | Font | Number | Alignment

Value (Y) axis scale

Auto

☑ Mi_nimum: `0`

☑ Ma_ximum: `2500`

☑ Ma_jor unit: `500`

☑ Mi_nor unit: `100`

☑ Category (X) axis

   _Crosses at: `0`

Display _units: `None` ▼   ☑ Show display units label on chart

☐ _Logarithmic scale
☐ Values in _reverse order
☐ Category (X) axis crosses at _maximum value

OK | Cancel

The *Scale* tab allows values to be set for *Mi_nimum* and *Ma_ximum* values, and *Major* and *Minor* units (the amount the scale increases by in each step).

In our example, changing the maximum to a more realistic 2,500 results in a revised chart as follows.

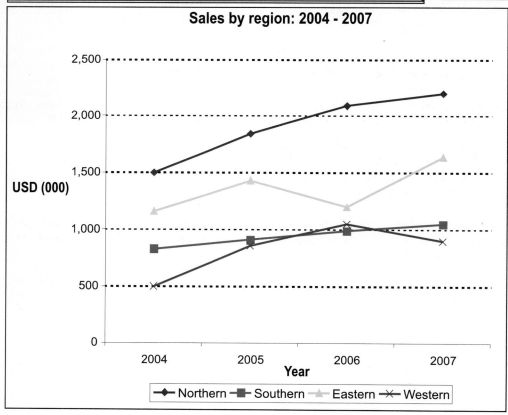

Sales by region: 2004 - 2007

USD (000)

Legend: ◆ Northern ■ Southern ▲ Eastern ✕ Western

Quick Quiz

Answer the following questions

1   A cell in a protected worksheet contains a formula. The cell is formatted as Hidden. When this cell is viewed on-screen, the cell will display as blank.

   Is the above statement TRUE or FALSE?

2   Which of the following, if applied as a custom format, displays a blank cell regardless of the cell contents?

   A   ...
   B   :::
   C   ;;;
   D   ###

3   What format is the data shown below in?

   ```
   UserID,Gender,Age,DateTaken,Score
   8248,M,39,17/01/2007,71
   8308,F,28,22/01/2007,64
   8306,M,32,17/01/2007,51
   8436,M,43,22/01/2007,44
   8231,M,21,22/01/2007,52
   ```

   A   Unicode Text
   B   CSV (Comma delimited)
   C   Text (Tab delimited)
   D   Not possible to establish from this extract

4   Cell A4 contains the value 99.49. Cell B4 contains the formula =ROUND(A4,1), and is formatted to display to 1 decimal place. Which one of the following is true in relation to cell B4?

   A   B4 displays 100; B4 actual value stored is 99.5
   B   B4 displays 99.4; B4 value stored 99.4
   C   B4 displays 99.5; B4 value stored 99.49
   D   B4 displays 99.5; B4 value stored 99.5

5   You've been asked to produce a chart that shows the proportion of the 'Total revenue 2007' figure attributable to each of the five markets your organisation operates in. The most appropriate chart type would be:

   A   Pie
   B   Column
   C   Bar
   D   Line

Answers to Quick Quiz

1   FALSE. The result of the formula will display in the cell. The Hidden format will prevent the cell contents displaying in the formula bar while the sheet is protected.

2   C. If applied as a custom format, three semi-colons ';;;' will result in a blank cell displaying regardless of the cell contents.

3   B. The data is in CSV (Comma delimited) format, as shown by the commas separating data fields (columns).

4   D. The ROUND function produces values that are different from those they are based on.

5   A. The most appropriate chart type to show relative shares of a single whole is a pie chart.

5 AUDIT

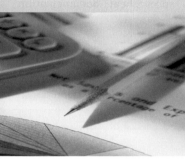
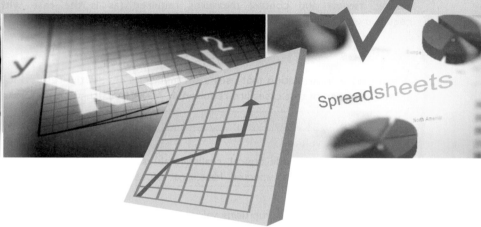

Measuring points

▸ Understand how spreadsheet criticality, risk and potential business impact determine the extent of review and control requirements.

▸ Submit the spreadsheet for independent review and approval before circulation.

▸ Recognise the need for periodic re-review.

▸ Run and validate test cases with typical and extreme values for all calculations.

▸ Check calculation outputs using alternate calculation methods.

▸ Un-hide rows, columns and worksheets.

▸ Un-hide formulas.

▸ Inspect formulas for logic and output accuracy.

▸ Recognise the presence of advanced features in a spreadsheet such as macros and pivot tables.

▸ Use IF function to test for cell values being within expected ranges.

▸ Review for data type mis-entry (eg text entry for numeric characters).

▸ Apply conditional formatting to highlight errors.

▸ Apply validation criteria: (values, whole numbers, and decimals).

▸ Apply validation criteria: (date, time and character lengths).

▸ Apply custom validation criteria.

▸ Be aware of data protection legislation or conventions in your country.

▸ Be aware that spreadsheets may need to be controlled as part of regulatory requirements.

▸ Recognise that spreadsheets may be controlled records and subject to archive requirements in legislation.

▸ Recognise the significance of disability / equality legislation in helping to provide all users with access to information.

SPREADSHEET SAFE™

| Setup | Input controls | Calculate | Output | Audit |

Testing and review

Testing and review play a key role in ensuring spreadsheet quality before release.

All spreadsheets should be tested and reviewed, before release, to ensure they operate as intended (ie to ensure their integrity). They should also be periodically re-reviewed as a check against unexpected changes.

The greater the risk of error and the potential business impact, the more formal and comprehensive the testing, review and control measures required (as is the case with spreadsheet documentation requirements referred to in Chapter 1).

Test cases

A test case is a calculation that uses a set input and checks the result obtained against the known correct answer. A range of test cases are required to ensure a calculation performs correctly under all conditions.

Test cases
1. Typical input values
Test cases should include typical, realistic values that you would expect to be entered. Results should be compared against those expected. Historical values and results should provide a good basis for comparison.
2. Extreme values
Test cases should also be run using values outside the range of expected inputs.
Examples of extreme values include:
▶ Large numbers, positive and negative
▶ Percentages over 100%
▶ Values with large numbers of decimal places
▶ Incorrect data type (eg text when number required)
▶ -1, 0 and 1 (useful as it's relatively easy to calculate the expected result)
▶ An error value such as #N/A
▶ Just under the lowest expected value
▶ Just over the highest expected value
▶ A very long number
▶ A space
▶ An empty cell

Test cases should be run for all calculations. A spreadsheet should be re-validated after changes have been made to the structure or formulas.

Alternate calculation methods

One way to check the validity of output is to use an alternate formula or function to perform the same calculation in a different way.

A useful checking mechanism in some circumstances is to use two calculation methods designed to perform the same result. If results differ, further investigation is required.

One example of this approach is the cross-check totals explained in Chapter 3. There are many situations where more than one approach is suitable. For example, if the formula =SUM(B5:B50*D5:D50) was entered as an array (ie entered using Ctrl+Shift+Enter) it could be used as an alternate check for the calculation =SUMPRODUCT(B5:B50,D5:D50).

Unhide rows and columns

To perform a complete review, the reviewer needs to see the whole spreadsheet (workbook). Any hidden rows, columns and worksheets should be unhidden to enable a complete review to be performed.

Hidden rows and columns can be identified by examining row and column headers.

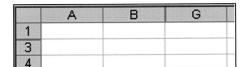

Row numbers jump from 1 to 3, meaning row 2 has been hidden

Column headers jump from B to G, meaning columns C, D and E have been hidden.

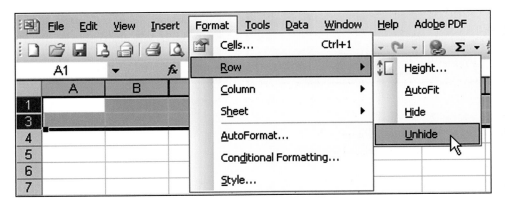

To unhide rows or columns, highlight the rows or columns either side of those hidden, and then select *Format* > *Row* (or *Column*) > *Unhide*.

To ensure all rows and columns are unhidden, you may prefer to highlight the whole worksheet (by clicking on the area above row label 1 and to the left of column A), then selecting *Format* > *Row* > *Unhide* followed by *Format* > *Column* > *Unhide*.

Unhide worksheets

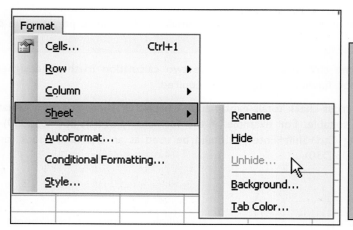

To establish if a workbook includes hidden sheets, select *Format* > *Sheet* from the menu (do this from within a sheet that is visible).

If the workbook doesn't include hidden sheets, *Unhide* will be greyed out (as shown here).

If the worksheet does includes hidden sheets, the *Unhide* option will be available.

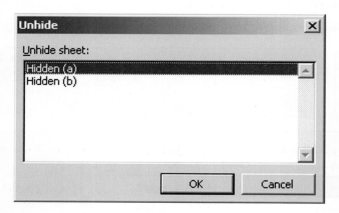

If *Unhide* is available and selected, a box will appear showing the names of hidden sheets for the active workbook.

To unhide a sheet, select it and click *OK*. Only one sheet can be unhidden at a time – so the process should be repeated until all sheets are visible.

Unhide hidden cells to reveal formulas

To reveal formulas held in hidden cells, follow the steps below.

1 This step is required if the workbook is shared.

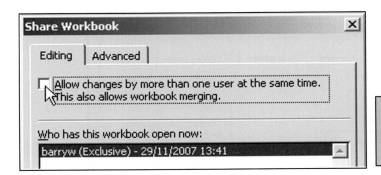

> If the workbook is shared, change this setting by selecting *Tools* > *Share Workbook* and 'un-ticking' the *Allow changes by more then one user* box.

2 Unprotect the sheet using *Tools* > *Protection* > *Unprotect Sheet*.

3 Select the range of cells to unhide. Then select *Format* > *Cells* and in the *Protection* tab, 'un-tick' the *Hidden* box.

We explained how to reveal the contents of a protected worksheet (even if you don't have the password) in the previous chapter. Refer to the 'Revealing hidden data: option 2' material in Chapter 4.

Inspect all formulas for logic and output accuracy

Inspecting a formula involves a close examination to ensure the formula does what is intended (ie it contributes correctly to the documented user requirements).

As explained earlier, testing plays an important part in ensuring formula logic and output is as intended.

Errors identified by Excel

Excel identifies formulas it suspects may contain errors by placing a green triangle in the top left corner of the cell (as shown in Chapter 3). The settings that control what Excel will suggest as possible errors are held under *Tools* > *Options* - in the *Error Checking* tab.

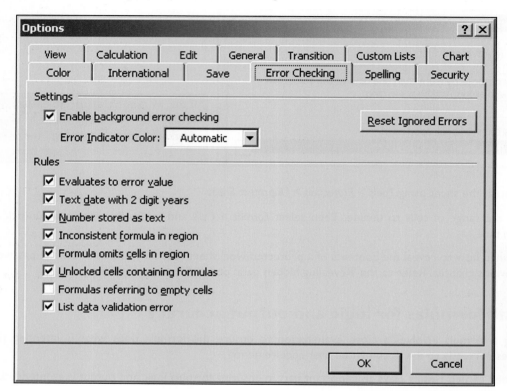

Excel will identify any formula that matches one or more of the 'ticked' rules as a possible error.

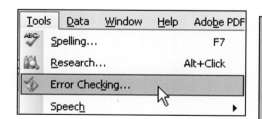

A worksheet may be checked for errors at any time using *Tools* > *Error Checking*.

This will not flag errors previously highlighted but ignored. To reset the error indicator on previously ignored errors, use the *Reset Ignored Errors* button on the *Error Checking* tab under *Tools* > *Options* (shown above).

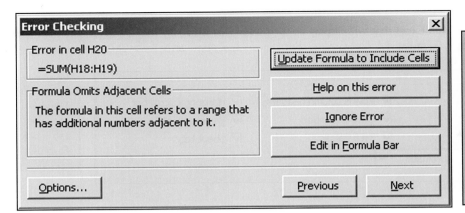

After selecting *Tools* > *Error Checking*, Excel takes you to each cell identified as a possible error. The error is described (eg *Formula Omits Adjacent Cells*) and options provided to update (amend) the formula or to ignore the error.

When all cells with identified errors have been dealt with, the error check is complete.

This error checking routine is a useful tool but should be used with care. Suggested corrections should be checked before being accepted. Remember also that only certain types of errors are checked for – a 'fully checked' sheet may still contain errors.

Display all formulas

There is a setting within Excel that will display all formulas. This is usually more convenient than clicking in each cell that holds a formula.

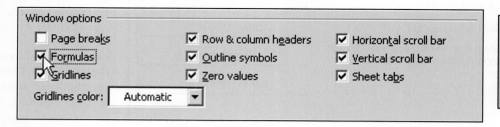

Select *Tools* > *Options* then in the *View* tab tick the *Formulas* box.

Inspect all formulas

Excel includes additional features to help inspect the logic of formulas.

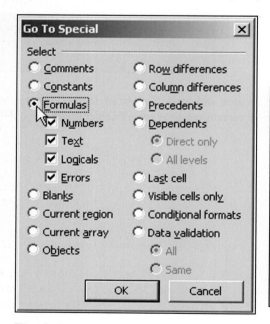

Select *Edit* > *Go To* and click the *Special* button. This brings up a range of options as shown.

To go to all cells that contain formulas, select the *Formula* radio button and tick all boxes. To only inspect *Formulas* with errors, tick *Errors* and un-tick the other options.

In the worksheet, use the Tab key to move between selected cells.

If groups of formulas should use the same logic, highlight the relevant range, select *Edit* > *Go To,* click the *Special* button and specify *Row* differences or *Column* differences. This will highlight cells that differ from others in the column or row.

The *Go To Special* window shown above may also be used to identify missing input values in a selection - by selecting the *Blanks* option.

The 'Identifying and correcting errors' material covered in Chapter 3 includes other error detection techniques, including use of the *Formula Auditing Toolbar* (the toolbar and individual auditing options are accessed via *Tools* > *Formula Auditing*).

Third-party spreadsheet auditing tools

There are a number of third party spreadsheet auditing tools available (eg XLSior, Compassoft). These may be useful, particularly for large, complex spreadsheets.

Indicate the existence of advanced features

Advanced features such as macros and pivot tables require specific skills to test and review. The existence of these features should be indicated in the spreadsheet.

Macros

As we explained in Chapter 1, a macro is a way of automating a series of actions. Some macros are relatively simple (eg recording a relatively small series of keystrokes), others form a relatively sophisticated 'program'. Macros are recorded in the Visual Basic for Applications (VBA) programming language.

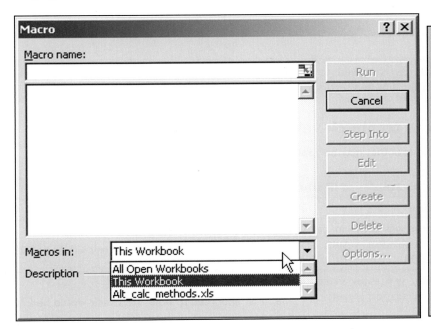

To check whether a workbook includes a macro, select _Tools_ > _Macro_ > _Macros_ and in the _Macros in_ box select _This Workbook_.

However, a macro that is used on a particular workbook does not have to be held in that workbook.

Selecting _All Open Workbooks_ in the _Macros in_ box will display macros in any open workbooks plus those in the users _Personal Macro Workbook_ – but doesn't provide any indication as to which (if any) macros are used with this workbook.

Macros need to be included in the testing and review process. If macros are used, this should be noted (eg a cell note or comment) within each sheet the macro will execute on. The note or comment should include the macro name and where it is stored, and also state where documentation explaining the role and workings of the macro is held.

Pivot tables

A pivot table enables different sub-sets of data to be extracted and viewed from a data set. If set-up correctly, pivot tables enable different views and summaries to be produced quickly, easily and accurately.

Pivot tables need to be tested and reviewed. The presence of a pivot table should be indicated in the sheet (eg a cell note or comment near to the table). Depending upon the size and complexity of the table, the comment should also state where documentation explaining the role and workings of the table is held.

Although pivot tables don't require names, giving the table a name reduces the potential for confusion in documentation.

Independent review

It is surprising how many errors or possible improvements could be spotted before a spreadsheet is circulated simply by having the sheet reviewed by a 'separate pair of eyes'.

The reviewer should understand the data in the spreadsheet and also be a competent user of Excel. To ensure that the review is unbiased, the reviewer should also be independent (meaning their priority is in ensuring the spreadsheet is correct).

Far better to delay circulation for the time this process will take, than to circulate a file containing errors.

Validation

A number of techniques may be used to check the validity of spreadsheet data. These include IF statements, conditional formatting and setting data validation criteria.

Using IF statements to check values

The IF function is a flexible tool that may be applied to test the validity of data.

Examples of IF statements to test data validity	
Situation	**Possible statement**
The result of a calculation will show in cell D20. Realistically, the calculation result is expected to be below 15,000.	=IF(D20>15000,"Too big?","") The most likely cell to hold this check would be E20.
The result of a calculation will show in cell D20. Realistically, the calculation result is expected to be above 5,000.	=IF(D20<5000,"Too small?","") The most likely cell to hold this check would be E20.
The result of a calculation will show in cell D20. Realistically, the calculation result is expected to be above 5,000 and below 15,000.	=IF(D20<5000,"Too small?",IF(D20>20000,"Too big","")) The most likely cell to hold this check would be E20.
A date is entered into cell E5. This date should never be in the future.	=IF(NOW()<E5,"Date in future?","") The most likely cell to hold this would be F5.
As explained in Chapter 3, totals in a table of numbers can be checked using cross-check totals. The two totals may be compared using an IF statement.	=IF(J10=J11,"OK","Cross-check difference") The most likely cell to hold this would be K11.

Identifying and correcting 'data type' errors

A 'data type' error occurs when Excel treats a value as a data type different to that intended. A common example is a number being entered as text.

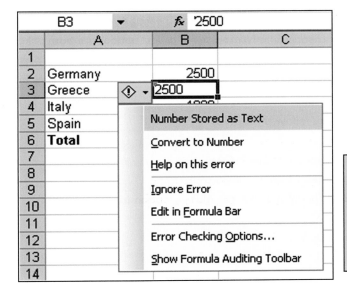

The total in B6 is incorrect. Cell B3 is left aligned and is also displaying a green triangle – these are clues that indicate problems with this cell. (Further explanation regarding Excel error identification was provided in Chapter 3).

In the formula bar we can see a single quote has been entered before the number. This tells Excel to treat this cell as text.

The on-screen menu option 'Number Stored as Text' provides confirmation.

Using ISNUMBER

		D3	▾		f_x =ISNUMBER(B3)	
		A	B	C	D	
1						
2	Germany		2500		TRUE	
3	Greece		2500		FALSE	
4	Italy		1000		TRUE	
5	Spain		4000		TRUE	
6	**Total**		7500			

The same error could also be revealed using the ISNUMBER function.

As shown here, =ISNUMBER(B3) returns FALSE, whereas tests on other values in the range return TRUE.

Converting numbers stored as text to numeric values

To convert the text stored in a cell to numbers follow the steps below.

1. From the Excel menu select _Tools_ > _Options_ and click the _Error Checking_ tab.
2. Ensure the _Enable background error checking_ and _Number stored as text_ options are both ticked.
3. In the spreadsheet, click on a cell with a green error indicator triangle in the upper left corner.
4. Next to the cell, click the error button and from the on-screen menu select _Convert to Number_.
5. Repeat steps 3 and 4 for all affected cells.

To convert a whole range of cells at one time, follow these steps.

1. In an empty cell, enter the number 1.
2. Click on the cell, then from the menu select _Edit_ > _Copy_.
3. Highlight the range you wish to convert from numbers to text.
4. From the menu select _Edit_ > _Paste Special_ and click the _Multiply_ option (under _Operation_).
5. Click _OK_.
6. Delete the number 1 entered in step 1.

Deliberately entering numbers as text

If numbers do not represent a quantity (eg they represent an account number, a credit card number etc), they should be entered as text. To do this, when entering the numeric code type a single quote (an apostrophe) as the first character.

This is particularly important for long numeric codes such as a 16 digit credit card, as Excel only handles 15 digits of precision.

Using conditional formatting to highlight errors

A conditional format is a font, border or shading pattern that is applied if a specified condition is true (as shown in Chapter 3). Conditional formats may be used to highlight conditions that are exceptional or likely to indicate an error.

	A	B
	Student ID	**Mark (%)**
1		
2	10183	67
3	10294	15
4	10352	63
5	10358	51
6	10433	88
7	10528	55
8	10552	171
9	10688	46
10	10761	43
11	10896	52
12	10997	-65

To apply a conditional format, highlight the relevant range then select *Format > Conditional formatting*.

In this example, the cells in column B (from B2 down) have been formatted to highlight values outside the expected range (between 20 and 90). Some highlighted values are definitely errors (eg 171, -65), other values are unexpected but may be valid, so should be checked (eg 15 could be the actual mark scored, or could be 51 transposed).

The formatting conditions applied are shown below.

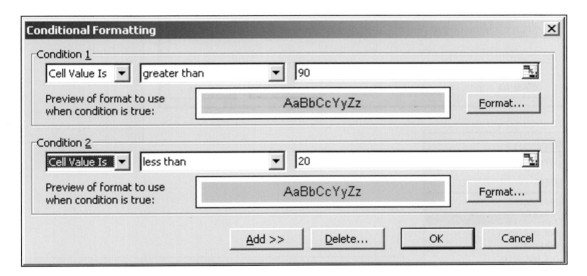

Although conditional formatting may be used to highlight input errors, it is perhaps better utilised to highlight valid values that display certain characteristics (eg marks over 90 that earn an 'outstanding') or to highlight an unexpected result in an output cell (ie a cell that displays the result of a calculation).

Rather than using conditional formatting to highlight input errors, a better approach is to reject incorrect values at the point of entry. Data validation (covered next) enables this.

Applying validation criteria to cells

Data validation criteria may be applied to cells to control the type of data that will be accepted.

Data Validation (Settings)

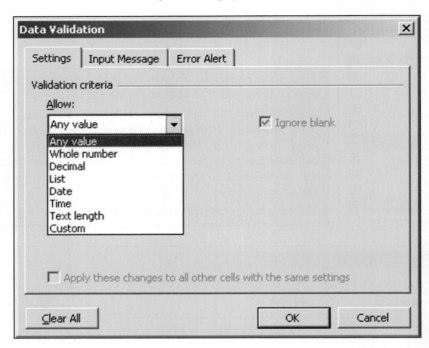

To set data validation criteria, first select the cell or cells the criteria will apply to, then from the main menu choose *Data* > *Validation*.

The Data Validation window has three Tabs.

The validation criteria are specified in the *Settings* tab, under the *Allow:* menu. A range of options are available to base the criteria on, as shown.

The *Input Message* tab allows a message to be set-up to display when the cell becomes active.

The *Error Alert* tab is where the action to be taken if invalid data entry is attempted is specified.

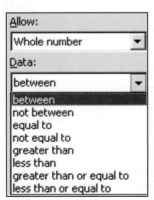

Looking again at the *Settings* tab, the *Data* menu (hidden by the *Allow* drop-down menu in the illustration above) is where details of allowable values are specified.

Validation criteria examples

Whole number

Allows only whole numbers that meet the value-based criteria.

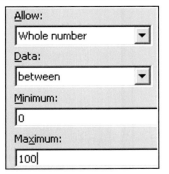

Decimal

As for whole numbers, but with decimals allowed.

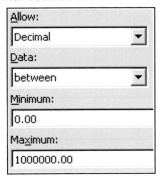

Date

Allows dates that meet date-based criteria (similar criteria options to the value-based ones).

List

Items from a list held elsewhere on the same sheet (or a named range of cells). Selecting *In-cell dropdown* enables the user to choose from a dropdown list.

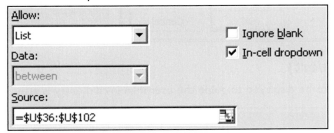

Text length

Allows text entry of a length that satisfies the value-based criteria.

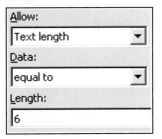

Other options

The **Any value** option allows all values to be entered. This could be used to allow any entry, but to provide an Input Message (covered later in this section) to guide the user.

Custom validation allows a formula to be specified that results in either true (valid) or false (invalid). For example if the text entered in cell B1 must start with the letter 'a', the custom formula: =left(B1,1)="a" could be used.

Custom validation facilitates flexible and sophisticated data validation.

Time

Allows times that meet the time-based criteria specified.

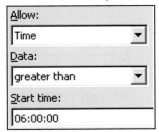

Data Validation (*Input Message*)

The *Input Message* tab enables a message to be displayed when the cell is selected, to help the user.

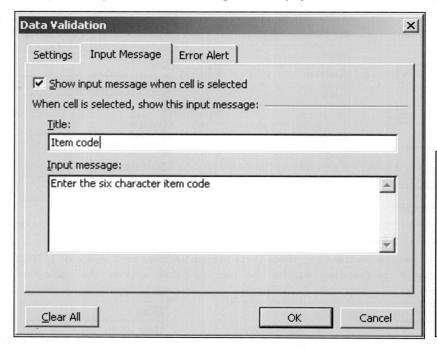

For example, if an item code was to be entered, and standard item codes have six characters, the message shown here would be appropriate.

This message could be used together with the settings shown on the previous page under 'Text length'.

Data Validation (*Error Alert*)

The *Error Alert* tab enables a message to be displayed to guide the user if an invalid entry is attempted.

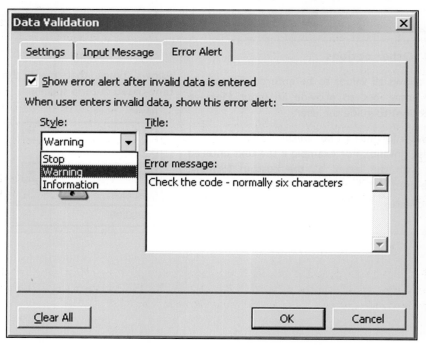

The error message should help the user by informing them of the expected format.

The *Style* setting contains three options.

Stop prevents the entry of invalid data – the user is presented with Cancel and Retry options.

Warning displays the message with Continue and Yes, No, Cancel buttons. Yes allows the entry.

Information displays the message with *OK* and *Cancel* buttons. *OK* allows the entry.

Using data validation

If cells are not locked and the worksheet is unprotected, data validation settings may be accidentally (or deliberately) removed.

Another limitation to be aware of is that data validation does not prevent invalid data being pasted (instead of keyed) into cells.

To highlight all invalid data in a sheet, choose _Tools_ > _Formula Auditing_ > _Show auditing toolbar_. If you then click on the _Circle Invalid Data_ button, cells containing invalid data will be circled in red (as in the example below).

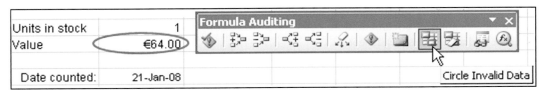

To find all cells with data validation, Edit > Go To > click Special, click Data validation, click All, and then click OK. Cells in the active sheet that have data validation criteria will then be highlighted.

Regulatory requirements

> Spreadsheet development and use may need to be controlled to comply with regulatory requirements.

Regulatory compliance is an important aspect of business. Organisations are subject to compliance regulations, legislation and statute laws that impose demands on how they may conduct business.

Using spreadsheets in regulated environments

Spreadsheets are often used in regulated environments such as the pharmaceutical and financial services industries. Regulatory requirements differ depending upon the industry, location and overseeing body. For example, in the US the Federal Drug Authority (FDA) is increasingly concerned with the use of spreadsheets in the pharmaceutical industry.

To comply with FDA regulations, spreadsheet development and validation has to follow a formal, documented development process. Design considerations include spreadsheet security, use of spreadsheet templates, location of regulated spreadsheets and Windows File System controls. The establishment and use of appropriate design layouts is seen as one way of ensuring the uniformity and testability of an organisation's spreadsheets.

Regulated environments often emphasise formal systems development processes for spreadsheets, including initiation, user requirements, documentation, testing, validation, maintenance and future enhancement procedures.

Sarbanes-Oxley (SOX)

The Sarbanes-Oxley Act is a piece of US compliance legislation, with global implications, which was introduced in 2002 (although many aspects came into effect late 2004). It aims to prevent financial malpractice and accounting scandals, such as Enron. It's often referred to as SOX.

One of the key sections is Section 404, which lays out the requirement for the management of a US public company to report annually on the operational effectiveness of the company's internal controls over financial reporting. This requires transparent and auditable systems.

The Act includes penalties for non-compliance - the Chief Executive Officer and Chief Financial Officer can be fined up to $5million, go to prison for up to 20 years, or both.

The impact of SOX on spreadsheets

In a US listed company (which may well have offices all over the world), any spreadsheet that could be interpreted as having any impact on financial reporting and control is subject to Sarbanes-Oxley. As such, these spreadsheets must be transparent and auditable. Many of the practices outlined in this book (eg logical design, meaningful documentation, comprehensive testing, independent review etc) help achieve a transparent and auditable spreadsheet.

Laws and guidelines

Retention of records

In many industries regulations and/or legislation require business records (whether paper or electronic) to be retained for a specific period of time. Organisations subject to these requirements must have effective an effective record retention policy that includes provision for archiving relevant spreadsheet files.

Data protection

> Spreadsheets may hold personal data that is subject to data protection legislation or conventions. You should be aware of the data protection legislation or conventions that apply in your country.

In recent years, as the amount of data held on computer systems has increased, privacy (the right of individuals to control information that relates to them) has become increasingly important. This has led to the development of data protection laws and conventions.

Spreadsheets that hold data about individuals are subject to these laws and conventions. Therefore, spreadsheet users should be aware of their responsibilities in this area.

Example – The Data Protection Act (1998)

Most countries now have legislation relating to privacy and/or data protection. This book uses the UK Data Protection Act (1998) as an example of 'typical' legislation. You should be aware of the legislation and conventions that apply to your country.

The Data Protection Act 1998 uses the following **terminology**.

▸ A **data subject** is an individual who is the subject of personal data.

▸ **Personal data** is information about a living individual, including facts and opinion.

▸ **Sensitive data** includes data relating to race, political opinions, religious beliefs, physical and mental health, sexual orientation and trade union membership.

▸ A **data controller** is the person or entity who determines the purposes and manner in which personal data is processed. A typical example of a data controller is an employer.

▸ **Processing** of data includes obtaining, recording, holding, altering, retrieving, destroying or disclosing.

The main points of the Act are:

▸ All data controllers (sometimes referred to as holders) must register with the Data Protection Registrar and must only hold and use data for the purposes which are registered.

▸ The processing of personal data is only permitted if the consent of the 'data subject' has been obtained, or to protect the vital interests of the subject or if processing is in the public interest.

▸ The processing of 'sensitive data' is only permitted if express consent has been obtained or the processing is required under law.

▸ Personal data should be relevant and not excessive in relation to the purpose or purposes.

▸ Personal data shall be accurate, up to date and not be kept for longer than necessary.

▸ Appropriate technical and organisational measures shall be taken against unauthorised or unlawful processing of personal data and against accidental loss or destruction of, or damage to, personal data.

▸ Personal data shall not be transferred to a country or territory outside the European Economic Area unless that country or territory ensures an adequate level of protection for the rights and freedoms of data subjects in relation to the processing of personal data.

The Act includes the following **rights for data subjects**.

▸ A data subject may seek compensation through the courts for the damage and associated distress caused by the loss, destruction or unauthorised disclosure of data or by inaccurate data.

▸ A data subject has the right to access personal data of which he or she is the subject.

▸ A data subject may apply to the Registrar for inaccurate data to be corrected or deleted.

▸ A data subject can sue the data user/controller for any damage or distress caused by personal data which is incorrect or misleading in relation to a matter of fact (rather than opinion).

Accessibility and equality

From both an ethical and legal point-of-view, computerised systems and the information held within should be equally accessible to as many legitimate users as possible.

Accessibility and equality is concerned with making services and resources (including information) available to everyone. The ideal is an environment which is accessible and user-friendly to all potential users, including those with physical, sensory or cognitive impairments or learning difficulties.

Example – The Disability Discrimination Act (DDA) (1995)

Most countries now have legislation that aims to provide equal access to information and other resources for people with disabilities. In the UK, the main legislation is the Disability Discrimination Act (DDA) (1995). We use this Act as an example of 'typical' legislation. You should be aware of the legislation and regulations that apply to your country.

The main aims of the Act are:

▶ To reduce discrimination against disabled people.

▶ To provide a right of access to goods, facilities and services.

The main points of the Act

The Act makes it unlawful for providers of goods and services direct to the public to:

▶ Refuse to serve a disabled person for a reason which relates to their disability.

▶ Offer a sub-standard service to disabled people.

▶ Provide or offer a service on different terms.

▶ Fail to make 'reasonable adjustments' so that disabled people can use the services more easily.

In some areas the Act has been amended or superseded by subsequent Acts and regulations. For example, the Special Educational Needs and Disability Act (SENDA) (2001) aims to clarify how the DDA applies to education providers.

Applying accessibility and equality principles to spreadsheets

Spreadsheet accessibility can't be considered in isolation. To access a spreadsheet, a user must first access a computer (generally a PC), operating system (usually Microsoft Windows) and spreadsheet application (usually Microsoft Excel).

Accessibility and equality considerations

1. Workstation location and design

For information held on computerised systems to be accessible, users must first be able to access a computer in an environment that allows them to work effectively. Building design, desk and chair choice, lighting, noise and other environmental factors can all hinder how a user interacts with a computer system.

2. Hardware

There are hardware options available that may improve accessibility.

▸ Keyboards with larger keys to help those who are visually impaired or have an unsteady hand.

▸ Compact keyboards with full size keys on a shorter base for those with limited arm, hand or finger movement, or who need to use the keyboard on their lap or wheelchair table.

▸ Different pointing device designs (eg trackball).

▸ Monitor size should also be considered.

3. Operating system

'General' options such as screen resolution and pointer device settings should be configured appropriately for each user.

Microsoft Windows also includes specific Accessibility features. In XP Professional, look under *Start > All Programs > Accessories > Accessibility*. After Accessibility options have been activated, an *Accessibility Options* icon should appear in *Control Panel*.

Facilities to help those who may have trouble reading text or data on screen.

▸ The Windows Magnifier (*Start > All Programs > Accessories > Accessibility > Magnifier*) splits the screen into two, with a magnified version of the lower part of the screen at the top.

▸ The Narrator (*Start > All Programs > Accessories > Accessibility > Narrator*) converts text including menus, dialogue boxes, icons and data into speech.

▸ *Control Panel > Accessibility Options > Display* tab includes an option to select a bold display scheme with larger menus, icons and mouse pointers.

▸ *Control Panel > Accessibility Options > Mouse* tab has an option to switch pointer movement and mouse control to keys on the numeric keypad.

Facilities to help those who may have trouble using the mouse and/or keyboard.

▸ On-Screen Keyboard (*Start > All Programs > Accessories > Accessibility > On-Screen Keyboard*) displays a standard keyboard on-screen, keys are 'pressed' using the mouse pointer.

▸ *Control Panel > Accessibility Options > Keyboard*. The StickyKeys option enables multi-key keyboard shortcuts to be input one key at a time, rather than simultaneously.

▸ *Control Panel > Accessibility Options > Keyboard*. The *FilterKeys* option means repeated accidental key presses will be ignored.

▸ *Control Panel > Accessibility Options > Keyboard*. The *Toggle Keys* feature switches on a bleeper that sounds when the Caps Lock, Scroll Lock or Num Lock keys are pressed.

Facilities to help those who may have trouble hearing.

▸ *Control Panel > Accessibility Options > Sound*. *SoundSentry* makes the caption bar, active window or desktop flash whenever Windows makes a warning sound.

▸ *Control Panel > Accessibility Options > Sound*. *ShowSounds* displays an on-screen caption for any sound made by the PC.

For an overview of the Accessibility features available in different versions of Microsoft Windows go to http://www.microsoft.com/enable/Products/chartwindows.aspx

Disability guides, tutorials, case studies and articles are available at: http://www.microsoft.com/enable

Accessibility and equality considerations

4. Application software

▶ As mouse use can present problems to some groups of users, **keyboard shortcuts** should exist that replicate mouse actions. Search for 'Keyboard shortcuts' in Excel's Help to see the shortcuts available in Excel.

▶ Excel includes **speech playback** to audibly read back data entered on a worksheet. The *Text To Speech toolbar* (see *Tools* > *Speech* > *Show Text To Speech Toolbar*) reads back data selected for verification. Or, the 'Speak On Enter' option may be used to hear the value entered in a cell immediately after entry.

▶ Excel can also use **speech recognition**, facilitating the use of dictated data entry and voice commands.

5. Spreadsheet design

Applying the general principles of good spreadsheet design and layout will help accessibility for all users.

▶ Consider on-screen and hard-copy **readability** issues when designing and formatting a spreadsheet.

▶ Pay particular attention to **colour schemes**. Factors to consider include colour clashes, glare, and the contrast between text and background. Overly patterned or tiled backgrounds should be avoided.

▶ Limit the number of **fonts** used throughout the sheet (ideally use one font only). Use relatively simple fonts, such as Arial, Tahoma or Verdana.

▶ To highlight text, use **bold** as this is easier to distinguish than text that formatted using italics or underline.

▶ In some circumstances, an organisation may need to provide **additional assistance**, for example making information held in a spreadsheet available in Braille.

Quick Quiz

Answer the following questions

1 Test case calculations should include:

  A Extreme values only

  B Typical values only

  C A mixture of extreme and typical values

  D Every possible value

2 A formula is required (in cell D5) that will display the text 'Check the quantity' if the value entered in C5 exceeds 20. Which of the following would achieve this?

  A =IF(C5>20,"","Check the quantity")

  B =IF(C5>20,'Check the quantity',"")

  C =IF(C5>20,"Check the quantity";"")

  D =IF(C5>20,"Check the quantity","")

3 Cell A5 has data validation settings that prevent values greater than 10 being accepted. Keying 11 into a different cell, copying this, then pasting to cell A5 would result in the value 11 being accepted.

  Is the above statement TRUE or FALSE?

4 Providing users with a dropdown list of valid values for data entry in a cell would most easily be achieved using:

  A A macro

  B Data validation

  C A pivot table

  D Conditional formatting

5 Which one of the following options correctly completes the following statement?
  The main aim of data protection legislation is to:

  A Protect the rights of data subjects

  B Protect the rights of data controllers who hold personal data

  C Protect the rights of people with disabilities who require access to data

  D Ensure all groups of users have equal access to data

Answers to Quick Quiz

1   C. Test case calculations should include a mixture of extreme and typical values. Testing every possible value is unlikely to be possible (or necessary).

2   D.

3   TRUE. Data validation does not prevent invalid data being pasted into cells.

4   B. Data validation (using 'List' and 'In-cell dropdown') provides this functionality.

5   A. The main aim of data protection legislation is to protect the rights of data subjects.

INDEX